C000132488

Taxi for Spirit

DIARY OF A SOUL RETRIEVER!

JEFFREY 'SHANTI' WOODCOCK

2QT Limited (Publishing)

First Edition published 2020 by

2QT Limited (Publishing)
Settle, North Yorkshire BD24 9RH United Kingdom

Printed by IngramSparks

Cover images: shutterstock.com
Taxi 'driver': Jeffrey Woodcock

A CIP catalogue record for this book is available
from the British Library

ISBN - 978-1-913071-87-5

Dedicated to all my soul retrieval 'teammates'.

Thank you, one and all.

Contents

Soul Retrieval: What is it?

SOUL RETRIEVAL IS simply the reconnecting of one part of a soul to the other part(s).

Let me explain by using my soul 'Shanti' as an example (Shanti is the spiritual name of my soul)

My soul is, and has been, on an everlasting journey of rediscovery of who and what it truly is:

A pure being of Love and Light.

My soul has visited this planet many times, having many experiences as it progressed, lifetime after lifetime. During my soul's journey it has experienced the darkest of times and the happiest of times, all causing my soul to experience every emotion possible on earth.

On some occasions the experiences have been too challenging for my soul, having experienced great discomfort and also happiness, leading up to the passing of the physical body.

Whether it be through love, fear, sadness or happiness, our soul can find it too hard to let go completely, so, part of the soul can become 'trapped' in the moment, so to speak.

In truth, it all boils down to one feeling: fear. Even

when passing in a happy state, a trapped soul may well choose to 'stay' because it fears there is nothing better than the happiness it has just experienced.

Over a period of visits to this planet, my soul has split into more than the 'odd piece', shall I say.

I know this to be true, for the healings I have experienced with my dear friend Yvonne has shone light upon many of these lifetimes, where she has ventured back to the place where a specific part of my soul has been trapped.

Yvonne has been instrumental in these lifetimes through many healings, and the information she has shared with me from these healings is now proving to be invaluable. With Yvonne's tutorage, I have attained the level of being able to learn of and visit these past lifetimes myself, so it's a win - win!

Thank you, Yvonne!

Here is one priceless example Yvonne shared with me:

During a healing, Yvonne was taken to Rosslyn Castle (not to be confused with Rosslyn Chapel) where Yvonne found my soul stand to attention near a ruined wall. Yvonne knew its true state was in ruins; however, my soul was trapped in an illusion. My soul believed it was still protecting a fully functioning castle.

Yvonne said to me after the healing, 'It took a while to convince your soul of this, but I did eventually.'

The outcome was that the part of my soul once trapped at Rosslyn Castle will have, through Yvonne's help, moved on, returning to heaven or a beautiful realm to recuperate before being safely reunited with the largest part of my soul at some point in the future – yay!

It's just like piecing together a jigsaw puzzle; no harm befalls our current physical body as we awaken to this phenomenon.

A soul retrieval can be experienced while we sleep, knowing nothing of it when we awake. On wakening, you may well begin to remember where your soul has been and what it has experienced.

It can also occur during a one-to-one healing session through any number of natural healing therapies, such as Reiki (many different versions of this modality), Shamanic healing, etc., as I experienced with Yvonne.

However, for me more excitingly, it can be done at the actual site of a historic/prehistoric event or at someone's home or workplace, which is why this book has been created, to share with you my many varied, wonderful, magical, amazing soul retrieval experiences.

Within this amazing 'team of angels' I am the conduit for heaven and earth, to bring both together, to help one or many souls return in one fell swoop.

When I am called to be of service in this way, I am in my element.

I simply *love* being of service in this way and, physical body willing, I would do this twenty-four hours a day, every day, for the rest of this physical body's tenure here on Earth. I would be a very happy bunny indeed! Alas, the physical body does need a little time to recover from the exertions of this wonderful work.

To help you become more open-minded of this type of spiritual experience, I wonder if you can relate to anything involving *déjà vu*.

This can be a fleeting moment, whereby you recognise a place, person or a clip from a scene in your life, until this very moment, having yet to be played out or a place or person you are very familiar with but know you haven't met in this present lifetime.

All these experiences point to previous encounters here on Earth.

I have had a few of these moments throughout my life but over the last few months they have happened more frequently; again, they are nothing to be fearful of. In fact, I find them very comforting, for I see them as signs that I'm on the right track as to my life's journey.

There are a few outcomes to these 'retrieval' experiences; all perfect.

For my part, I know that whatever I am meant to do I complete my 'mission' as it were, during any soul retrieval, via many signs which appear to confirm this. There may well be souls who choose to stay, simply because another soul retriever has agreed to reconnect with them at the appropriate time.

There is also a scenario whereby the soul can become trapped while the physical body is still alive and healthy. This occurs when a physical body experiences great trauma, shock, fear, loss, etc. in any life experience.

This I refer to as an 'essence'.

Essence: this is simply the residue of a person's memory which, over time, will create a build-up of specific emotions and feelings in a specific place. The longer a person – or any number of people – have stayed in one specific place (for example, where they have lived) these essences become stronger, especially if their experience is powerful enough emotionally, mentally or physically. Most of the time it will be a combination of all three.

Any situation which creates enough, fear, drama or trauma for the physical body, can cause part of our soul to 'stay put' – the soul will opt for safety!

Again, as with all other forms of soul retrieval, I will add my experiences of this type of situation in this book too.

Another way soul retrieval can be necessary occurs when we form an attachment to close friends or family, who we love so deeply that when they pass, we can subconsciously hold on to a part of their soul which holds them here on Earth. We don't consciously know this until a time when we are spiritually aware of this type of experience or when the trapped soul is ready to 'move on'.

However, when this happens, it is for us to let go; for this part of our loved one's soul is ready to move on, especially when they start to make noises, etc., getting our attention, very clearly and loud in some cases hehe!

When I do a soul retrieval of this nature, I specifically explain to the person/people who have called me that while it's necessary I assure them they will still have a connection to their loved one(s), but a healthier one.

This is their 'reward' for allowing the soul they have attached to, to move on and return to the light or to heaven to be healed. When a soul retrieval is completed, this part of the soul can then reconnect to the main part of their soul, wherever it may be and whatever it may be experiencing. Sometimes the soul will be taken to a healing temple to receive healing, etc., before coming back into the fray, so to speak.

In truth, this is what soul retrieval is all about.

It's all about Shanti, the 'soul' part of our union if you will. He is on a journey; Jeffrey plays his part too (as the vehicle for the soul) and like any good team we both have our gifts complementing each other's.

✱✱✱

Here are a few pointers to make reading this book easier for you:

Soul(s) ~ this is my chosen term for those trapped, there are other terms you could use if you wish, such as 'spirit' or even 'ghost', but I must stick with one term and follow it through, so that no confusion befalls you.

When I say soul(s) I do mean only a *part* of their soul(s) because the soul itself can be dissected into many parts and become trapped in many different lifetimes along its journey.

This is an important piece of information to take in when reading further into this book.

I know this may be a tad confusing but the title for the book sounds better with the word spirit rather than soul.

This is the only time I will use the term 'spirit'.

SR ~ this is short for 'Soul Retrieval'.

EC ~ this is short for 'Essence Clearing'.

Move on ~ this is the term I have chosen to use for the trapped soul(s) leaving this planet.

Other terms, such as 'going home', 'going back to the

light', or 'going back to heaven' may be more comforting for you to use in place of 'move on'.

As the SR experiences multiply, so does my wealth of knowledge, which you will obviously see through the explanation of each SR as my experience and confidence grows.

> Helping trapped souls move on and find peace
> is an honour to behold; I am so blessed.
> This is my soul purpose.

Also, during the course of this book, I make one or two references to a book entitled *Darkness Was, As Light Is Now...* this will be coming out shortly after this one!

So, without further ado, please read on!

Whitby B&B ~ 8th May 2012

THIS WAS MY first real experience of SR. I hadn't a clue what was happening throughout the night and early morning. (My angelic friends reminded me to add this piece, because of the experience I gained from it!)

The hotel I usually stay at while in Whitby was full, so I had to look elsewhere, ending up in a Bed & Breakfast; a lovely B&B, with a charming landlady called Jackie.

Jackie gave me a tour of the B&B and gave me the choice of two rooms. I had full use of the kitchen; basically, I had the run of the B&B as I was the only one staying there, and I would find out why this was later in the evening.

While in the kitchen, Jackie mentioned she and her partner had only just bought the house and opened it as a B&B. The elderly lady she bought it from was selling up, her husband having passed away very recently. Jackie pointed to the spot where the elderly gentleman passed away; in the kitchen, while sitting in his beloved rocking chair. When standing in the exact spot, it felt like I was in a freezer, so cold was it!

At this time, I had no idea whatsoever about SR so I simply thought no more about it. I went out for a walk, returning in the evening, when things then started to get 'eventful', shall I say. I was quite tired from my journey to Whitby and then from the walk, the sea air, etc., so I thought, as you do, that sleep would be imminent... How wrong I was! It was 5am before I finally nodded off.

Prior to that, my mind was in constant disarray with all sorts of thoughts running through my mind, which led to me ring Dad around 3.30am because I really thought something had happened to him. Thankfully, nothing had happened but he was quite perturbed at the time of my call. As I say, I finally fell asleep at 5am but only for a few hours; I was wide awake at 9am but absolutely shattered.

I went downstairs into the kitchen for a drink and found myself stood in the spot where the rocking chair once sat, this time there was no coldness to be felt. I knew then that the gentleman had moved on. I didn't know where he'd gone, I just knew he had.

The SR was over and I knew absolutely nothing about it.

I did get some information from my friend Yvonne during a healing I had with her a few days later, however. I was told the house was empty other than me staying there, so my soul could do its work, helping the gentleman safely move on, but also that I wouldn't wake anyone up prior to me going to sleep.

I needed to be so tired that when I fell asleep my soul was able to do what it needed without fear of me waking up. This was all quite overwhelming for me but as I write this piece, I feel so blessed to have been a part of this experience; priceless!

I had played my part without knowing what I was supposed to do; such is the amazing 'team of angels' who are a massive part of this SR team.

As I look back now, it shows how far I have come regarding my journey, and how my experiences are now standing me in good stead for the next period of my SR journey, of which you will read about within these pages.

William Wallace's Cave ~ 30th June 2017

THIS WAS THE first SR when I knew what was going on hehe!

I left Pathhead, near Edinburgh, only a few miles from my destination: Rosslyn Chapel. I have been to Rosslyn quite a few times over the last few years, so it was a surprise when I got lost. Yes, I had to find where I was via a map on my phone. Surprisingly, showing me, I was quite close.

On closer inspection of the map, my focus was taken by the words 'William Wallace's Cave'. I felt I had been guided here to be made aware of this historical place and then visit post haste.

It was off the beaten track, so to speak. I drove down a lane, only to be met by two houses, one a B&B. I knocked on one door and politely enquired as to where the cave was and how to get to it. The gentleman said, 'Go past the other house, through the gate and down a very steep incline through a wooded area,' also adding, 'be very careful as it has rained and the path will be very slippery.' He wasn't joking!

I thanked the gentleman and headed past the house

and through the gate. I soon came across steps which had been carved into the landscape then carried on further down turning into a dirt track; it was very slippery indeed!

Nearing the cave I slipped, sending a bottle of water spinning out of my hand. I was fortunate to stop just before I ran out of path; the drop was over a hundred feet straight down, phew! I dusted myself down and continued to the cave's entrance.

As I entered, the cave was quite small. I looked around for a moment or two then out of nowhere I asked all my angelic friends to help assist any trapped souls within this cave to move on – I had no earthly idea what I had done.

I was, however, being asked to trust Archangel Michael and my other angelic friends, by doing and saying what I thought apt, coming via their guidance; a perfect team performance, hehehe!

Having finished, I made my way out of the cave. Just a few steps outside of the cave, there was a ledge with a silver butterfly and a silver five-sided star staring me in the face. I took these divine gifts as confirmation I had followed my guides 'to the letter', bringing about a positive outcome. In what way I wasn't really sure, but through these gifts I knew I had done what I was guided here for.

This was the first of what I now know to be many wonderful experiences, doing what I truly love doing: a win-win situation – and now for more experiences!

Edinburgh 'City of the Dead' Tour ~ 12th July 2017

DURING A HEALING with my dear friend Yvonne, I was blessed with an excitable feeling; I needed to go to Edinburgh and take in the City of the Dead Tour, and did so a week later!

As I was soon to find out, this was another opportunity to face some fears along the way. As the tour began, the guide explained where we were going and how it could be a little claustrophobic for some and quite dark in places, which pressed a few fearful buttons within me, shall I say, but which I quickly shrugged off.

During the tour, the guide also mentioned if anyone was to stay down there for over forty-five minutes, suffocation was a distinct possibility. I felt a little uneasy hearing this too!

As I entered the vaults, the fear of any claustrophobia disappeared. The further we went into the vaults, one in particular, the guide reiterated the possibility one could suffocate if staying down there too long. I started to feel a real unease, my throat tightened, I felt sick and a little light-headed but I persevered. I knew I was here to 'work' so I continued onwards.

The guide mentioned a soul who resided in these

vaults, a soul which had been named 'Imp'. I suppose it was a name the soul had been given, due to its antics when others had been on the tour. As soon as the guide mentioned the 'Imp' I felt tingling all down the back of my body, head to toe. I knew immediately it was the Imp. I also felt similar connections throughout the tour.

Again, I asked my angelic friends to help any trapped souls move on. We moved through a couple more vaults, which led the group back into the open air! The tour ended.

I spoke to the guide and explained to him about trapped souls, hoping it would help in some way. I felt this was as much for me to overcome my fears regarding telling others what I had done, via the SR, but it's all a learning curve.

The 'Imp' Soul Retrieval (SR) Conclusion ~ 4th February 2020

TODAY'S EXPERIENCES HAVE somewhat unexpectedly, yet magically, brought an ending to this SR. I was unable to sleep this morning, with so much information coming to me for various issues, this being one of them.

A soul has been making itself known to me over the last week or so but wouldn't give me any information, as if 'he' was playing with me! I didn't know it then but it was the Imp. On Saturday, while shopping and waiting to be served, I noticed a lady had just opened up the till next to me; she invited me to go over to her. I did simply because I would, and did, get served quicker.

Now, here's the thing...

As the lady, Viv (an alias), served me we got talking about the price of my purchases which came to £6.66. I said to Viv, 'This number has a different meaning to me, different to what many people believe it to mean; the number of the beast!' For me it was a sign from my angelic friends to trust what information is coming through regarding this SR.

The conversation was very brief, because there

were people queueing behind me with their purchases. However, during our chat, I had been close enough to Viv to allow a soul, who had been with Viv for however long, to 'latch' onto me.

I felt a little sickly on leaving the store but didn't connect the dots until this morning. I first came to realise the soul with me was indeed the Imp. I then sensed a little apprehension regarding how our friend the Imp would react to the lady's soul from the supermarket. A few hours later I found out in no uncertain terms!

While taking some rubbish out to the bin, being outside for only a matter of seconds, the door somehow locked all by itself!

Mmm, very strange indeed!

Strange because the door needs some amount of force to close it, let alone lock it. Again, I understood it was a two-fold message:

1. It was the Imp making himself known to me, confirming my thoughts were correct and that I would know it was him when receiving more information.
2. He simply locked the door because he didn't want the soul of Viv to be in the house.

Obviously, some sort of forgiveness was required from both sides but more so from the Imp. I did get back in the house, having taken the keys out of the lock when I opened the door; something I never do, yet, boy was I glad to find them in my pocket!

Anyway, back to the SR. The soul, nicknamed the 'Imp', had played various tricks on past tours and earned this title, but I have come to understand this was the Imp's nature when alive. He was a trickster or even a con artist, without making any judgement of him, because as I saw in those vaults, it was a very unpleasant way to live, so I can fully understand someone doing anything they could to make their life a little more bearable.

Alas, the Imp played one trick too many while alive and paid the price, with his life. The soul of Viv was the cause of the Imp's passing, through some unpleasant actions. Obviously, he had done something to cause anger to Viv's soul so much so that the outcome was death.

The Imp didn't do it on purpose, it was simply his way! Something he will learn from, now he and the soul of Viv left this plain for pastures new this morning during the SR 'hand in hand', which was beautiful to be part of.

Yet again, my angelic friends have blown me away with another magical way in which a SR can be completed and over a period of years, too!

Whitby Abbey and St Mary's Churchyard (Whitby) ~ 27th July 2017

HAVING ENTERED THE Abbey, I circled the outer areas of the abbey itself before inviting my angelic friends to join me. As I stood in the main part of the abbey looking at the large window, I just said what came to me regarding the SR.

This all happened very quickly, so quickly I thought I had missed something, but as I was leaving the abbey via three flights of steps, I received a clear sign I had done all I was asked to do, via the number of steps in each flight.

Each had nine steps; for me this was a clear sign!

The number 999 is a sign for me that an ending/completion has occurred; there is more to the number but this was how I saw it. This SR was also a sign for me to trust that whatever I did or said would always be perfect!

This was soon followed by what I thought was more SR work in the adjacent St Mary's churchyard. I walked around the perimeter of the churchyard, but felt no souls connect with me for retrieval purposes;

I am always guided to walk around the perimeter if it's feasible. However, I was guided to find a double gravestone with a husband and wife next to each other.

As I read the epitaph, I became more and more amazed with their experiences... These are just the factual dates, etc. (I did take a picture of the gravestone.)

- Both man and wife were born on the same day: 19th September 1600.
- They were married on the 19th September (no year was displayed).
- They had twelve children!
- And they both left this mortal coil within five hours of each other – yes, you've guessed it: on 19th September 1680!

The further I read into these words, the more I tingled!

I felt I had to add this to the book because it was such an amazing experience, filled with such love!

Flodden Battlefield, Northumberland 1st Visit ~ 1st August 2017

I HAD FELT the urge to visit Flodden over the last few days, so here I was in the car park, readying myself for what I thought would be a straightforward day's experience.

I purchased a map of the site (putting some money in the box next to the maps) and proceeded to visit the areas I was guided to. Within minutes my feet were wet; my shoes weren't the best for field walking but hey, they couldn't get any wetter now!

I moved into one of the fields named the 'killing fields'. I feel it explains itself. I walked up the first side of the field only to be set upon by midges (flies) attacking me from all angles.

During this unprovoked attack, while flailing my arms around trying to keep the flies at bay, my phone fell from my pocket; I didn't know this until sometime later.

At the top, I then went left and across the field, by this time I had become quite frustrated regarding the fly experience. I then made my way down the other side of this field, which had to be done via the road.

Now standing at the gate which would lead me back into the field, I knew my angelic friends were urging me to enter, so I could encircle this field completely. But after the experience with the flies and obviously something else niggling inside me, I didn't feel I wanted to walk along this path.

However, when I get this feeling, this is exactly what I need to do, to bring about a true completion to any 'challenge'.

Half-way across the field, I stood still.

I spoke out loud, calling on any trapped souls to embrace the help which had guided me there, to help them move on. My angelic friends were ready to escort any souls as and when they were ready to leave this 'field of illusion'.

Having finished my speech, I began to see flashes of the battle which took place on this and surrounding fields. I felt the atmosphere, the heaviness of much fear and despair; these emotions were too much for me, they brought me to tears.

I know, in part, that this was my soul connecting to a past-life experience, but I also felt useless, unable to stop this battle, to stop the waste of many lives, and to what end?

Having done what I felt necessary, I headed back towards the car park, stopping on the way to take a picture of the field I had just circumnavigated, only to find my phone gone! Usually when something like this happens, I can sometimes become quite annoyed, however, this time I just thought *well, I need the phone*, so off I went, retracing my footsteps, leading me up the hill once again.

Fortunately, a man and two women were coming down the hill, so I asked them had they found a phone. One of the ladies said, 'A man had found it,' pointing out the man's house as she spoke, I thanked the lady and headed off in that direction!

As I neared the car park, a lady approached me and asked, 'Are you Jeff?" I said, 'I am.' She gave me the phone and said her husband was waiting in the car; they were setting off to do errands.

Now this is the magic of this experience; the man's name was Roy, which just happened to be the same as my dad's!

What are the odds on that?

However, this is just the beginning of this amazing retrieval work here at Flodden; I would return in the near future.

Flodden Battlefield, Northumberland, 2nd Visit ~ 14th August 2017

MY RETURN VISIT was as magical as my first but in different ways.

I parked the car at the other end of the village, knowing on arrival, this was the area I was being guided to walk around and work on. I set off on foot around the perimeter of the battlefield; another area where fighting took place.

During my walk, I entered an area where I felt great emotional pain. I stood a while and allowed my thoughts to come clear but nothing materialised, so I carried on. Throughout the walk I was 'guided' to talk to the souls trapped here. So, I did as guided and I spoke aloud, asking them to forgive their foes and themselves for what had occurred here. I felt this would ease their anger towards each other, allowing them to move on en bloc as it were! Which I do feel happened.

I sensed as Archangel Michael and all the other angels played their part, the portal of light witnessed a mass exodus from these fields. The souls walking into the portal side by side as friends rather than enemies, having put their differences aside. Having left the field, I now walked back into the village via the road and back to the car.

I thought to myself, *I wonder if the people who live here can feel the difference or sense something has happened?*

I soon got a message from my friends: it doesn't matter what people feel of sense, it is simply for you Jeffrey, to trust what you have done has helped this world heal in a wondrous way, thank you!

It's for me to do my job, enjoying it immensely as I do, but without becoming egotistical about it.

Point taken!

Flodden Battlefield, Northumberland, 3rd & Final Visit ~ 6th November 2017

ARRIVING AT BRAXTON, where Flodden is, I walked up to the memorial cross, which overlooks the battlefield.

I asked Archangel Michael why he had brought me back here. He said nothing but simply guided me to look over at the killing field, having played my part on the first visit, helping the souls of the battle move on.

During my first visit, the field felt so heavy and sickly with negativity; only natural with the amount of souls who were trapped here from this battle alone. Archangel Michael said, 'Look at the field you walked around on your first visit.'

As I looked at the field, I saw new life had sprung up where heavy negativity had once resided. This was all created for me to see and realise what part I was playing, to help this world heal. Tears flowed; I felt so very humbled by it all!

I am simply blessed to be of service in doing what I do, it doesn't matter if anyone living in the surrounding areas feel or know that something has changed, it's purely for me to be and I am grateful for this role, knowing I have made a difference in positive ways.

James IV of Scotland (Flodden) SR (Additional Information) ~ 14th & 15th August 2019

THIS EXPERIENCE BRINGS closure in all ways to this amazing SR. This morning I was roused from slumber, feeling a very strong presence around me.

Prior to this, I kept hearing a song by Big Country called 'The Storm'. Now, whether this song was written about Flodden or not, I cannot say, but it did awaken memories within me regarding Flodden as I listened to it. I soon came to realise it was part of my soul, who in this lifetime was James IV.

The part of my soul which had become trapped at Flodden, reconnected with me when I visited a second time, right in the very spot where I stood for a little while feeling the deep emotional pain wash over me.

(I have since learnt, in the last few months (2020) that I have no need to bring souls or essences back home with me, as you will read of further in this book, but we learn as we go along.)

I felt, when standing in the hollow where James IV was killed, he had let his countrymen down. I felt he blamed himself for the disastrous loss they bore at Flodden. I also felt that at the time of his passing he felt utter despair, again because of the result at Flodden.

So, not only did I connect with the trapped soul, I also connected with all the emotions that arose within this period leading up to the battle and his death – this is what I have explained at the beginning of this book regarding an essence. The ever-increasing discomfort James IV experienced of having to do something he didn't necessarily want to do but as king he had to show leadership, strength and faith, and to stand up for his countrymen and women.

This part of my soul, James, has been with me since the 14th August 2017, two years to the day!

It has taken my soul, perhaps me, this long to forgive and let go of what 'we' believed we had caused 'our' loyal subjects to experience: pain and suffering with no end result. In truth, we didn't do any of this, simply because every soul involved chose to be part of this experience, as part of their soul's journey/learning, call it what you will. Only now do I fully understand this!

But I have also come to understand there's a natural order as to how things unfold, and while this part of my soul has been with me, it has been necessary to deal with other issues before James was able to move on.

Everything happens within the realm of
divine timing!

Back to the morning I was roused from slumber. After an hour of talking to my soul (James), coaxing him into letting go, I became very tired, so I told James I was going to sleep and that Archangel Michael would leave the portal open, so there was no rush, he could just take his time and go when he was ready.

A few hours later, I woke up and asked was James still there, I got no reply. This I took as my confirmation that all was well.

Another weight off of my physical shoulders, for with each SR on a personal level, it removes heavy negative energies which have lingered since these souls first became trapped and attached to me!

Lockerbie, Scotland ~
29th August 2017

TRAVELLING SOUTH FROM Rosslyn Chapel, fear began to rise from within me, however, I was gifted some crumbs of information. I was told I was heading to Lockerbie to do some SR for those souls from the air disaster in 1988, and any other souls who had walked this ground many, many years previously.

Before my arrival, I was guided to view various internet sites regarding this disaster, to get some idea of where I may be visiting. As guided, I only took the information on board which resonated with me.

One area I visited was a churchyard near where a part of the plane landed; I just had a quick walk around then return to the car. Looking at the map where the wreckage once lay, I decided to drive the whole way around, completing a large circle, too far for me to walk. I felt this was enough to connect the angels to any trapped souls. If it wasn't, my angelic friends would have taken me back; thankfully, whatever I did by driving around in a large circle was enough, for now.

By this time, I was back in the town, being guided to the street where the wings of the aircraft caused such damage; around fifty people died here, including eleven residents who were oblivious to this most unpleasant experience which was about to turn their world upside down.

This is where the information gets even more amazing!

As I parked my car, facing the street, a car with 888 on the registration plate came towards me. I took this as a sign I was about to do some SR, my take on this specific number at this time. As I walked down the street, fear surfaced, really powerfully this time. Still I had no idea what this was all about, so, I continued to walk to where the memorial was situated.

Having found the memorial where three houses once stood, I felt the presence of souls around me. I began talking to the souls explaining, as I have on a few occasions when called to do this line of work, that there are many divine angels with me here to help them move on, reuniting them with their loved ones, etc.

Having done all that I felt drawn to say and do, I then made my way back to the car; this all happening within ten minutes.

As it began, so did it end, with a car driving past me with the number 888 on its registration plate as I sat in the driver's seat! This time I took the message to be: 'Your work is done, Jeffrey'.

This SR has also involved, in part, my soul and a very recent past life, residing within one of those people who were so drastically affected by this experience. He never recovered and as I believe his life ended via suicide; he survived the crash but almost all of his family didn't.

This terrible experience was so recent that my physical body, Jeffrey, was alive at this time having his own experiences with another soul residing within his body. When the time was right, the soul of the person in Lockerbie left and entered my body.

I will explain this now.

There is a situation which can occur where a soul exits one physical form to reside within another physical form. When a part of a soul's journey ends, it may choose to leave and find another body to continue its journey of rediscovery of self.

This happened to Jeffrey in 1999 – this is what we call a 'walk-in'.

Culloden Battlefield, Scotland, 1st Visit ~ 3rd August 2017

AGAIN, THIS SR was to be completed in two visits.

The first visit I arrived with a broken bone in my foot, rendering me slightly incapacitated regarding walking!

On reflection, I feel this initial visit was to prepare and seal the inner area with a ring of light, where it seems most of the fighting took place, preparing it for my return in the near future.

However, as I walked the inner area, I took it upon myself to invite any souls present who were ready to move on, saying they now had an opportunity to do so. I saw headstones of the many Scottish Clans who had come together to fight for what they believed in.

I stood at one particular headstone, I can't remember which clan, but I just felt what a waste it was; a very solemn moment for me but knowing I was to return at a later date I took this as a positive.

The broken bone in my foot really did the trick because I wanted to do so much more to help these souls here.

Patience was required!

Thankfully, I didn't have too long to wait for my return to manifest!

Culloden Battlefield, Scotland, 2nd Visit ~ 20th & 30th October 2017

I RETURNED TO Culloden to be welcomed by the cold and fine rain.

I began this SR by walking around the perimeter as much as I could; there was about ten yards where I was unable to complete the circle. I held the intention that it would be sealed trusting this was sufficient.

As I started the SR I focused on a small building which was used as a form of hospital. I walked around it twice but was unable to get inside. I feel this was where part of my soul had become trapped.

I then moved around the perimeter in an anti-clockwise direction as far as I could, and then had to double back on myself a little before continuing in an anti-clockwise direction.

As I progressed, there was a beam of sunshine peeking through the clouds, the further I progressed the brighter and slightly larger this beam of light became.

I saw this as being the portal for the trapped souls to step into when they were ready. Half-way round I stood for a moment, contemplating my next move, only to be brushed passed by two deer, I could almost touch them so close were they; amazing.

Almost at the 'finishing line' I met a gentleman with two dogs; a local of this area. We had a very brief chat and then went our separate ways. Only a few steps had I taken when I had the strong feeling that the gentleman's soul and my soul had fought on the very spot we had just met!

As I write this, I am going very tingly, a reassurance regarding this as truth. I looked up and said something like, 'God, you never cease to amaze me,' so blown away was I.

I finished off this amazing SR thanking all the help I had and returned to my car. I felt there had been a major evacuation of this field by many souls through the efforts of the SR team I'm part of, but there may well be some souls who chose to stay, awaiting another person to come and connect with them via SR.

Each soul has its own unique journey and has soul contracts with other such souls but every one of them will be set free in time.

Now back at the car, I looked up at the sky above the battlefield, seeing the portal at its brightest, a very profound moment for me, and another sign I had done all I was asked to do; very humbling indeed, and oh, the rain had stopped as well!

True Love's Set Free, Culloden ~ 16th to 18th October 2019

THIS FINAL PART of the Culloden saga began in earnest, on Sunday 13th October 2019 with Debbie, my dear friend, giving me two series of *Outlander* to watch.

On Wednesday morning I felt drawn to visit Gawsthorpe Hall near Burnley, in the north west of England. I was ushered there via a 'conversation' with a lady who resides in Newchurch, but a few miles from the hall, saying that the hall had some link to the Pendle Witches.

The message from the lady was, in part I feel, to stir my curiosity, as I have written about a SR done in and around Pendle regarding a part of the Pendle witches' history.

Arriving at Gawsthorpe, I felt a connection to spirits, in the car park and then a little later near the toilets; on reflection I feel these were nature angels making themselves known to me! Having then been around the house, in every room, I felt peace and serenity, apart from one bedroom which was cold as I entered. However, this coldness wasn't enough to confirm I had connected to a trapped soul.

On leaving I did feel a little downhearted, for in these situations I sometimes feel I have an expectation of how this day and other SR days will go, only to experience them in a totally different way altogether!

I was perplexed at why I had been guided to this beautiful hall, but soon received the answer while watching the first episode of *Outlander*.

Outlander is a series based around a lady who ends up going back in time, through a portal at a stone circle in Scotland, therein experiences life in 1743, the time prior to and during the Jacobite rebellion. Up to now, she has been unable to travel back to her original life in 1948. As she begins to accept that she is trapped in this reality for now, she falls in love with a laird. They marry and the relationship soon blossoms into a very deep, loving one.

A real true love story!

Now, I know I have connected to a part of my soul at Culloden, on the battlefield, and felt my soul had a partner, also involved in this lifetime. *Outlander* has reminded me of similar experiences me and my true love shared in the past life at Culloden.

All reminders bring up quite strong feelings and emotions; I felt at times during the series very cold, as if I was in an icebox, so cold was it. The coldness varied over my body. My right side was the coldest but my left side was also very cold too, signalling to me that I had the presence of a male and female – both shouting out at me, 'Time for us to go home!'

As I say, the series showed me the depth of love shared between the two main characters, akin to my soul and his true love in the lifetime in Culloden.

The female 'energy' only appeared after my visit to Gawsthorpe Hall, so however strange it may seem, something happened there which, having been completed now, was allowing this next piece of my soul's jigsaw to fall into place.

So, on the Thursday evening I readied myself to do a SR for these two 'love birds'. With the initial SR I spoke to them both briefly, explaining what will happen if they accept the guidance from me and my angelic friends.

Having done this, I bid my friends farewell and went to sleep, in the hope that by the time I woke up, they would be back in the arms of 'God' enjoying their rewards for a job well done.

Alas, on waking I felt their presences were still with me.

I lay back in bed and began to talk to them in a more detailed, yet calm manner; in these types of SR where my soul is asked to let go of past experiences, it has been, and was, tough to do so, especially when it involved someone I loved.

This is why they were still here, as well as blessing me with further information I would require to finish this SR.

The lady's soul is a soul from my soul group, meaning it was a very strong, close connection. We have experienced many lifetimes where I thought she was my true love, only to be wrong.

We have experienced lifetimes where my soul was her 'protector', and lifetimes where I was jealous of other souls spending time with her in relationships, trying to regain her attention by doing outrageous things, never succeeding.

We have had lifetimes experiencing romantic relationships but they never succeeded in being the experiences we both sought. The lifetime in Culloden was the epitome of true love, albeit with one or two conditions attached! The love we had for each other was so very strong throughout, and through whatever we faced in this Culloden lifetime.

This was the reason why they were still here with me in the early hours of Friday morning. I realised Shanti/Jeffrey was finding it hard to let go, but eventually we did.

On waking up later that morning (Friday), the two 'love birds' had successfully transitioned back to heaven, knowing they had to let go and allow each to go their own separate way here on in.

Confirmation came via a song I was singing upon waking, called 'Welcome Home', by Peters and Lee.

But now in this lifetime both myself and my friend's soul knows the truth, that we are souls on a journey and until we let go of this lifetime, neither of us would be able to settle into a relationship until this issue was finally put to bed.

Thankfully, it now has, and boy what a difference I have felt since they moved on!

Pictish Fort at Burghead, Scotland ~ 3rd August 2017

THIS WAS A very swift visit.

The Fort itself is all but gone. However, as I have come to realise, while I was guided there specifically by the fort's history, indeed wherever I'm guided for any initial SR, there will have been the soul or souls from this era of history but to remember this.

People, animals, birds, etc. have lived in this area and all areas of this world for thousands, nay millions, of years.

With this awareness, I have connected with souls from many periods of history – not just the eighth-century Pictish fort or Culloden battlefield, etc. – which makes the SR even more exciting for me, while also feeling so honoured to be doing 'God's' work in this way.

Whatever souls I connected to while at the fort, they were swiftly helped on their way as I looked out to sea, a beautiful way to end their self-imposed incarceration.

'Medium' S.O.S. ~ 9th November 2017

I VISITED WITH Zoe (an alias) who I had been chatting with on Facebook, saying she was being harassed by a particular soul, so, while I was in the neighbourhood, so to speak, I offered to go and see if I could help.

Now, having arrived at Zoe's we chatted, leading me to understand the trapped soul was a gentleman who had connected with Zoe at her last home. Zoe was quite fearful of this soul and of other 'goings on' in her home; Zoe had been a practicing Medium but had become fearful of what others had told her, so stopped.

Having understood the complexities of this connection between Zoe and the gentleman's soul, who I have named Tony, I began to talk to Tony in a calm and loving manner. Tony was in a state of confusion, so, there was nothing to be gained from judging whatever a soul or human does or has done, for it is all a part of our soul's journey.

I spoke at length with him but nothing seemed to appease him. Having done my best, I bid farewell to Zoe, saying if anything came to mind I would let her know.

Having returned home and gone to bed, I then woke up at 1.45am, having had a very vivid dream; my soul having travelled to do some 'astral' SR work. I returned to sleep, but was then rudely awakened by the TV standby button flashing vigorously on and off; a soul trying and succeeding to get my attention, hehehe! This was around 3am.

Now awake, I felt the energies of this soul around me, so asked for a name. I didn't vocally hear the name but felt it was Tony from the day before. I said, 'Is that you Tony?' I went tingly all over; there was my confirmation!

Obviously, Tony had attached himself to me as I left Zoe's, knowing he was ready for 'home' and that I was the person to help him achieve this goal.

As I talked, I felt a knowingness within me, I felt Tony was seeking forgiveness from Zoe over an unresolved past-life issue.

I sat in silence for a while until feeling the need to call upon my angelic friends, to oversee this SR.

It was for my soul, Tony's soul and my angelic friends, to escort us back to Zoe's home, to converse with Zoe's soul, her 'higher self' rather than the physical being named Zoe. This was brought to a successful conclusion. Zoe's higher self forgave Tony and immediately Tony's soul was escorted back to the light.

(I then realise all the above paragraph had happened during the SR, the deed already done, so to speak!)

The reason I woke up a second time was to understand what had happened and write down the events of the SR, to pen in this book. By the time I had done this, which happened very quickly I may add, the time was 3.13am. My confirmation came, strangely yet magically, via Yvonne, my dear friend.

Around 9.30am I was sifting through Facebook, only to see a post added by Yvonne simply saying: 3.13!

I had known Yvonne for twelve years at the time this experience occurred and never once has she posted only a specific time. The only explanation: it's gotta be 'divine magic', hasn't it?

Well, it was certainly good enough for me!

Zoe felt the soul was attaching itself to her, while all the time it was Zoe, through her fear and unresolved unforgiveness which was keeping Tony here. This is one way a SR may seem to fail.

In truth, in all SRs divine timing plays a part.

If it isn't time for a specific soul or souls to move on or, as in this SR there had been Karma to balance before the soul could go home, any prior SR work will be preparing the soul for the perfect time to move on. Another amazing piece of insight to add to my ever-growing knowledge of SR!

Thank you, Angels!

'Circle of Light', Scarborough ~ 21st November 2017

FROM WHITBY I headed to Scarborough, needing to sort some banking issues out. As I entered Scarborough, I took the scenic route along the seafront, then into the town centre to park up.

While here I was reminded of my last visit here with Dad and his friends, this seemed like years ago but did bring up some emotion to let go of. I concluded my business and headed back to Whitby, only after roadworks and a detour had taken me around the outskirts of Scarborough in the other direction.

A few minutes later, I arrived at the same roundabout I had turned left at a few hours earlier, I felt there was some significance to this day but couldn't put my finger on it. It was only when back in Whitby I realised that I had gone full circle around Scarborough's main town centre and holiday areas.

Archangel Michael said I had been guided to act as a conduit to place a 'Circle of Light' around the area, while driving; no reason was given.

Again, having understood what had occurred, I simply felt blessed to be of service, even in these circumstances; no SR being done, for now!

Perhaps we were setting this area up for a later visit? Who knows, watch this space!

Scarborough SR Revealed ~ 27th December 2019 to 9th January 2020

DURING A DREAM experience this very morning, I was shown a music deck and on it a record, but it was revolving in an anti-clockwise direction, revealing a hidden message.

The message: John Byron Salvation.

The dream ends!

As I awoke from this dream, I felt a presence with me, quite strong down my left side. I asked the soul, 'Are you John?' Immediately, I went tingly all over, signifying a 'yes' to my question.

I had been for a long walk the day before and had ventured into an area I hadn't been before. I thought logically I had connected with this soul during my walk but as the conversation went on, I found this wasn't the place of original contact.

I did – as I normally do – ask many questions without giving the soul time to properly reply, so I left it there and was now in the process of waiting patiently for further unforced pieces of the jigsaw to avail themselves.

However, having retained some patience, I received

the information a few days later; the life I write about occurred in Scarborough, hence the reason behind my adding this piece after my original SR work in Yorkshire, via the Circle of Light.

Additional guidance and awareness came to me via a film and a television series, with both showing me a child being born to a father not married to the mother.

For whatever reason, this was my soul's choice of experience in the Scarborough lifetime. This also involved the souls of a friend who I go walking with, her husband and a friend of hers who has recently passed over.

Last year, my friend went to Scarborough with her husband for a holiday, unaware they would also connect with John during their visit, and had brought him back home; this is how 'God' works, amazing eh?

The next step occurred while my friend and I were out walking. This gave John the ideal opportunity to switch from my friend to me, so I could take things to the next level, being able to understand the connection, the feelings and signs I was receiving since the switch took place.

A perfect example of this book's title: *Taxi for Spirit*!

My friend was the 'taxi' for John, from Scarborough to her home, then I became the taxi for the last part of John's journey before he and the other trapped souls were able to move on from this world; amazing!

John then made himself known to me, via the dream experience, the record playing backwards, etc. Why this way, you may well ask?

Well, I believe it is another way my angelic SR friends wish to share with me, regarding how SRs can be done.

These divine words from my angelic friends, 'Many routes to market' sum it up perfectly, thank you!

I'm being shown many different ways, so I will never tire of doing SRs. I can, hand on heart, say this will never happen but feel my angelic friends are helping to keep me fresh, so to speak!

The SR itself took place later the same evening that John had transferred from my friend to me. It happened while I slept, because there were a few issues to be resolved with the other souls involved, so my guides thought it best for all concerned.

So, I spoke to John beforehand, reassuring him he had done nothing wrong, that he was loved, asking him to forgive himself, etc. Another variation of a chat I do with any trapped soul who connects with me, especially those whose actions have caused unpleasantness to others.

During the SR John sought forgiveness from the husband; he sought forgiveness from the child and also from the mother who bore the child. The mother was also seeking forgiveness from her husband and the child for her actions, which had caused great sorrow when this issue came to light in that lifetime.

Both John and the mother/lover, during the SR, were blessed with an opportunity to forgive themselves for their actions, because love can take many forms. They acted on their feelings, as we all have done at one time or another.

Both were invited to let go of any guilt, so they could fully allow the healing to take place. The father was being asked to forgive them both, as was the child.

I woke later the same morning and felt John had

vacated my room, signalling a completion of this magical SR.

I really love the ending, simply because it signifies that peace has replaced a myriad of other negative emotions, a gift we all benefit from!

PS: Because my parents in this present lifetime have also been my parents in other lifetimes, I had assumed they would have been my parents in all other lifetimes but this isn't the case, as shown by this SR – again, such a priceless insight for me!

My soul was the child in this lifetime!

Dad 'It's About Time', Whitby ~ 9th December 2017

THIS SR BEGAN as I watched a film, funnily enough, called *About Time*.

The film was about a family where the men were able to travel back in time, to experience past events over and over, allowing them to create the perfect experience or simply because it was a happy moment.

The part where the father had been diagnosed with cancer and his eventual passing affected me the most. His son, even though his father had passed, was able to revisit past events to spend time with his dad. However, when the son's wife had their third child, this brought an end to the son's ability to travel back to spend time with his father.

When the father told his son, 'this would be the last time [he] could visit', I was in floods of tears, because it reminded me of my enforced exile from home and Dad. I only saw Dad briefly once before he passed a year later; it wasn't for a lack of trying, that's for sure!

I didn't get to say I loved Dad, and it broke my heart that I wasn't there, to be with him as I had always prayed and hoped for. My life with Dad has been written about at length in the book entitled: *Darkness Was … As Light Is Now!* (If you wish to find out more about this and other experiences!)

The film ended, I started to sense Dad was with me, but urging me to invite Archangel Michael and the angels who help with the SRs. I finally realised; I had held onto a part of Dad's soul here since he passed!

The love I had for Dad created an attachment; any attachment we form with anyone or anything will create unhealthy scenarios.

I knew I had to call in the angels to help Dad's soul move on for healing and then to be reunited with the other part of his soul. My word, it was hard to do but oh so necessary, for both dad and me!

I asked Archangel Michael to help Dad's soul move on, knowing this would elevate our relationship to a higher level, a relationship where unconditional love is present.

Having concluded Dad's SR, I received a short message from him, saying simply: 'IT'S ABOUT TIME'.

As Dad jokingly said this I visualised him with a smile on his face and taking his words as confirmation. A lovely ending to a very challenging SR.

For me personally, the SRs I have done for my immediate family and soul family are the toughest to do, by far!

Church of St Oswald, Lythe near Whitby ~ 28th December 2017

I VISITED LYTHE Church of St Oswald near Whitby, going back to the tenth century and an important Viking burial ground.

Entering the church and to the left there was a display of Viking relics, photos, etc. As I looked around, I felt a coldness around me, I knew this was a soul; the soul of the Viking? My dad's friend, Bill, told me there is a grave of a Viking but I didn't find it for some reason.

I feel so blessed to be part of something so special, to be of service in helping my fellow brothers and sisters return home so they can continue on their divine journey.

As I have said before, I rarely see any visual effects of soul(s) moving on, but my role is to be the conduit for Archangel Michael and his legion of light angels and any other divine angels who are a part of this amazing SR team.

So, as I walked around the perimeter of the church and graveyard, feeling various levels of coldness, I began to speak in a way which will best ease those souls who were ready to move on. I stood still, almost in the centre of the graveyard, and continued to call any souls to head into the portal my SR friends had created until I felt those souls who were to move on had done so.

Sometimes I don't really know what I'm doing, but I trust whatever I say or do, is exactly what needs to be said or done, which then allows Archangel Michael and the other SR angels to play their part, bringing complete success to this magical experience.

I feel so much joy when I know we as a team have, through our actions and words spoken, caused a ripple of positivity. Whether it's one soul, or many, I feel blissfully happy for them and their loved ones; priceless!

A Mental Asylum in the USA ~ 30th December 2017 & an Old Mansion in Ireland ~ 6th January 2018

(Both 'visited' as I slept)

MY SOUL IS also now being used 'in service' as I sleep.

I have been roused from slumber twice in a week, instantly remembering where my soul has been.

The first such experience occurred after I had watched a ghost hunting programme on TV.

This episode was based in the USA about a mental asylum which was deemed to be a very dark place to visit. Numerous patients over a long period of time had passed while residing there, in unpleasant ways, causing souls to become trapped, along with a build-up of negative fear-based energy.

I woke with a vision clear in my mind; I had connected with part of my soul and was shown a vision of him being set on fire while in a cell. It was a prison in all but name; the patients were treated unpleasantly to say the least.

Whatever SR work was necessary, it had been done while I slept and although it was a very swift SR I was left with a nasty taste in my mouth, regarding the way my soul had been treated.

Thankfully, the SR was completed while my soul/Shanti and our SR teammates were there at source, so to speak. So, I must forgive those who caused my soul distress in that lifetime, which I was able to do.

My soul was off on his travels just a few days later, to a haunted house in Ireland, and again on waking, I knew we had been doing SR work, feeling so blessed.

Both these visits have connected to parts of my soul and have been dealt with, while there. In the Irish SR I received very little information as to what happened. I obviously didn't need to know regarding this SR.

Having had these two new experiences, I felt a modicum of disappointment, in a good way, for I would have loved to have actually been there to experience the whole thing in a physical sense.

However, as Archangel Michael so perfectly explained in his unique and loving way:

Beloved Jeffrey, there is not enough time for you physically to visit each and every site, we will take you to so many magical places which I believe will keep your passion for this work simmering for a lifetime
Love Michael

Family Feud Ended ~
9th January 2018

THIS SR OCCURRED while in Whitby.

I got to sleep around 2am, waking at 4am, being roused from slumber by a very gentle, yet cool spirit brushing against my face, as if to say, 'Come on, Jeffrey, please wake up, you've work to do.'

I came to, from a very deep sleep indeed, taking me a few minutes to fully regain consciousness. I asked who was with me? I got no immediate answer, but I did begin to receive thoughts which fitted in perfectly with this current issue: the receipt of some photos.

The photos were kindly sent to me by my auntie a few weeks previous, photos of our family a long time ago. I asked, was this soul connected to the photos? 'Yes,' came the reply.

I then began to name people in the photos, such as my dad, my nan and granddad, etc., hoping for a sign when naming the person involved. As I named my family members in the photo, a name I had never even thought of came to mind, my uncle Ian, who I haven't seen for over forty years; I can't recollect if he was even in the photo!

Dad and he didn't see eye to eye, if you know what I mean, their relationship was similar to mine and dad's – very stormy with very few moments of calm!

From this point on, everything I write happened while I was asleep.

Shanti, my soul, was guided to Uncle Ian's, to mediate for both Dad and Uncle Ian's souls to help bring a marvellous, joyful and peaceful ending to their soul contract. I began to converse with Uncle Ian, telling him that whatever had happened, whatever he had caused others to experience while he was in a physical body, it was coming from a place of pain within him. 'Please know you did nothing wrong!'

I asked him to forgive himself for what he thought he had done wrong, to offer forgiveness to his family members, to know he is loved more than he can ever imagine while residing in a human body. And to know he was worthy of this joyous blessing.

As I talked to Uncle Ian, I felt a presence so strong join us. It was so powerful it would have knocked me off my feet, had I been standing, such was the power of this angel.

I soon learnt it was Dad; amazing!

Now, Dad's only desire was to help his brother heal this part of their life experiences together, preparing Uncle Ian whenever the time comes for him to move on. Uncle Ian would know no different or feel no different on a physical level after this meeting occurred but thankfully, his higher self did.

It was so beautifully poetic; it really made my heart sing with joy.

I called upon Archangel Michael and his band of

amazing angels to bring their karma back into balance. Forgiveness at a higher soul level had been attained, yay!

Additional explanation of the above SR:
It has taken Dad just over three years to heal adequately since he moved on before this coming together of family was able to take place, to ensure a positive outcome for both. Had they come together at an earlier time, Uncle Ian wouldn't have been ready for this healing to take place – again, everything happens within the realms of divine timing.

Things would have still been physically tense between Uncle Ian and Dad, on Uncle Ian's part, even though Dad was now in soul form.

While one soul is still residing within a physical body and the other soul having transitioned back into soul form, a healing needs to occur on some level for a peaceful outcome to be possible especially when the physical being/body is in a dark place regarding his or her emotions, anger, frustration, 'poor me' syndrome, etc.

I know Dad has been working with Uncle Ian since he moved on to help Uncle Ian heal sufficiently to accept this.

While experiencing these emotions the physical being isn't in a place which is conducive for a reconciliation to take place... Thankfully, a wonderful resolution was attained!

I was also blessed with additional information about Dad and me; a similar issue Dad had with his brother and my Uncle, Ian! This concerns a feeling I have had throughout this lifetime with Dad; Shanti (my soul) has also had his fair share of lifetimes revolving around this too. Feeling I was second best.

With the above SR done for Dad and Uncle Ian, this issue, which had until now been well hidden from view, the 'green-eyed monster' of emotions – jealousy – has also been healed; a true bonus for them and for us all!

My grandad, in Dad's eyes, favoured my uncle Ian rather than Dad. Dad always felt that whatever he did to gain his dad's attention, it was never enough.

I have felt exactly the same with my dad, feeling I have been competing with my brother Jack, who passed away before I was born; subconsciously feeling the need to be better, when in truth this is completely unnecessary.

On an ancestral level, this issue goes back through a few generations!

So, due to the healing experienced by Dad and Uncle Ian and my awareness of the soul and its journey, between the three of us we have brought this ongoing issue for our ancestors to an end, yay!

Metheringham:
'A Village Forgiven' ~
14th to 19th February 2018

As I APPROACHED the village, a fear surfaced quite suddenly, powerful enough to make me question whether was I in the right place?

I had, for the previous month, been talking to Jo (an alias) a lady who lives in the village. The connection was familiar and yes, I did think she – as all the other ladies I have connected with – was my true love, alas not to be; but that's another story for another time!

However, for this SR to take place the feeling that romance could well be in the air needed to be strong enough to get me to visit Jo, which was a pivotal part of this amazing and true experience.

Arriving in 'Meg' as the locals call it, it was raining, a sign a cleansing had already begun.

I met up with Jo on the Wednesday and Thursday, spending time with her, getting to know her.

Things felt good, yet they changed dramatically after Thursday evening.

Her daughter met me and Jo in the pub where I was staying. We had a really good chat and a few drinks, which in those days was very rare for me, but again I felt the drinks enhanced the evening, in readiness for what was about to surface over the next few days.

When meeting Jo on the Friday, something had changed regarding our connection.

I now believe my angelic friends created this scenario with Jo to get me, not only to visit Meg but to stay for the duration, which would last five days!

So, for me to feel there was a possibility Jo could be the 'one' gave me the incentive to stay longer than I would usually, I would never have visited this place otherwise.

As you will learn in the coming paragraphs, I needed to spend every second I had here in Meg, and for a very good reason. Indeed, Jo was pivotal to this whole experience.

Friday evening, I did something I never really do; I went for a late-night walk.

I found myself being guided to walk around the inner village rather than around the whole village, and while doing so I felt such dense energy, heaviness I have never experienced before.

As I walked around the inner village the fear began to show itself in the form of anticipation. I sensed the whole village was waiting for something to happen, no idea what but they felt it was an unpleasant experience, as did I.

I actually entered a Chinese take-away, just yards into my walk. I had no idea why because I had only moments before had a meal in the pub. I found myself standing there browsing the menu with no intention of ordering anything.

However, as I know now, it was necessary for me to be standing still and in the very place I believe the young boy was 'manhandled to death'. By being still, I allowed the trapped soul, the part of my soul Shanti, time to attach himself to me, so we could carry out this SR.

As I walked around the village, a lovely and peaceful village, it was strange to see so many houses with security lights at the front of their homes. It may have just been me but it was very strange indeed. Jo had also told me that when out dog walking, the locals don't allow their dogs to mingle, which again I found a tad strange.

I received guidance that the people of this village were, subconsciously awaiting the return of a soul who had lived here back in the 1500s, who was blamed for a fire which gutted almost the entire village!

Yes, it was my soul, Shanti.

My soul resided within a child during this lifetime and was blamed for starting the fire!

I wasn't shown the full vision of how the child was dealt with, but it was a very unpleasant one, which ended with the child passing in much pain. My soul, in the form of this child, vociferously vowed to return and seek revenge for the wrongdoing which was taking place.

Jo told me some of the ancestors from the time of the fire were still living in the village, generation on generation!

This explained the heaviness I felt during my walk around the village – fear of anticipation or waiting for this soul to return and heap untold misery on this village.

This was a different experience for me, for when I have done 'God's' work on battlefields, graveyards, etc., the extent of the fear lasted only as long as the battle prevailed or the souls had been killed. The negative energies would have stayed at the same level rather than multiplying.

This experience was different because the ancestors of those who live there now saw and caused the situation, whereby the child sought to gain revenge for the wrongdoing which occurred.

They heard the child's threats, from which, they started to nurture, as I call it 'anticipatory fear' which multiplied as the days, years and generations passed!

Until I, Jeffrey, was at a level to cope with this SR and my soul able to forgive those actions against 'him' (the child) in this past life, would we have returned!

This was the fear I felt as I approached Meg, the fear of what we were entering into, preparing me in advance. When arriving, those still living there were subconsciously awaiting their nemesis to return. Thankfully, what the villagers feared didn't materialise.

Instead, the whole village was blessed with a cleansing and healing from this past experience!

So, the spiritual understanding for me had reached a level where forgiveness was attainable, rather than revenge, but more importantly those other trapped souls who were still in the village, from the fire and other periods from the past, were blessed with the opportunity to move on via my angelic teammates' help.

Again, the SR was done on the evening walk.

I didn't realise this until the day I was to leave. The rest of the time was gathering information to help me understand the nuances of this situation, which have been amazing!

On leaving Meg on the Monday morning, I got a message from Jo saying she 'had never seen the village as quiet and peaceful as it was at that moment.' My cue to take this message as my conformation of a job well done and so thoroughly enjoyed!

Whenever I bring an end to an ongoing personal issue or as in this case a SR for a village, a wave of peace comes over me, or the area involved.

I or they had taken in a very deep breath and finally let go of all the tension and stress that I or they had been holding on to for the duration of the issue/situation.

The calm is the next and final step to completion. I or they, by relaxing allow our bodies to recuperate, and when this period is done a new energy will emerge bringing more light into any personal issue or area involved.

Whether the villagers felt anything energetically is no concern of mine, for I must and do trust that when doing any SR I know I will be guided to leave only when we have played our part as a SR team.

First Contact with 'Black Magic' ~ April 2018

I'M A LITTLE unsure as to the specific dates when this issue came up but it has been so beneficial to have had this experience...

It all came about when a friend told me about a lady who was experiencing some unpleasant goings on in her life. A few days later, I went with two friends and conducted a thorough spiritual cleansing of the house, feeling this had done the trick.

A few days later the lady got back in touch, with the end result I stayed with her for a few days, which helped us both out. My short stay was long enough to bring up such fear within me; it was a challenge to stay put for this time.

During one conversation, the lady spoke about things that had gone on in the barn regarding her 'ex'. When the phrase 'black magic' was uttered for the first time, I went into panic mode.

Thankfully, after a few hair-raising moments, I calmed down, hearing these words from my guides: 'There's nothing to fear, it is simply a build-up of negative energy.'

Over the next two days I ventured into the barn where the horses were stabled and felt some energies in there but nothing untoward. The lady's grandson arrived the next day and came with me into the other barn, asking me what did I see/feel?

He had obviously seen some of the things that had gone on in this barn. I saw nothing but did feel quite unnerved while there. I don't think the young man was impressed with my answers but I told the truth.

When coming out of the barn, I felt very wobbly on my feet and shaking all over; I had connected to the energies but had forgotten to ask Archangel Michael for protection.

Later that day, I did ask for a cleansing from those very negative energies.

I spoke with the lady the next day, coming to the conclusion I had done all that I could regarding this issue. The lady was nurturing fear because the situation was still being played out, shall I say; her ex was still living in the area, so the fear was a little like the Meg SR in some respects. I feel she was anticipating a return of her ex!

Completely understandable, but as I have stated in other SRs, if a person is still holding on to any soul or essence of a soul, especially through fear, this will take some healing. Only when the person is ready to let go of the feeling/emotion will completion be attained.

I was obviously guided here to experience black magic and gained invaluable insight during it.

I did feel disappointed I was unable to successfully clear this area but then realised this is all part of doing SRs – sometimes things don't go as I/we would like.

Another invaluable lesson learnt!

'Black Magic' Circle, 1st Visit ~ 24th November 2018

THERE ARE FOUR parts to this SR, which will make sense when having read them all, I hope, hehe!

A friend and I went for a walk at Rivington Pike, in the dark! Not something I was overjoyed about doing if I'm honest but knew it was something we needed to do.

As we walked, I had a very clear vision of highwaymen on a stagecoach, a surprise because until this moment I hadn't experienced a vision as clear as this, amazing!

We walked on a while when a choice was to be made, left or right?

I asked Gina (an alias), 'Which way are we going?' I didn't want to go right, but knew we had to. Gina confirmed my first thought by saying, 'Right.'

About fifty metres down the path I veered off into the thickening grass and trees. Gina said it felt quite eerie. I stopped to get some kind of connection with the area, when Gina said she could see twelve 'figures' in a circle.

With Gina's vision I asked her to guide me around the circle helping to place a ring of light around the circle itself. This was necessary to surround the dense negativity which resided there, boxing it in, so to speak.

Gina then stood well back from the circle, mentioning the twelve figures. I immediately said, 'Thirteen,' and then stepped into the circle, asking Gina to guide me into the centre.

It was a place where black magic and human sacrifice had taken place; a lot!

While I was stood in the centre of the circle, Gina said that I changed 'form' a number of times, while calling Archangel Michael and my other guides to help with this SR.

The twelve souls around the circle left with a modicum of ease! I saw these souls leave in a puff of black smoke heading upwards but the man leading proceedings didn't want to go.

I thought he had right at the end but was wrong, as I would find out a day later. I then brought the retrieval to an end.

Gina and I walked a bit further just to gain some composure, for it was quite a sinister place to be in the dark. I felt there was a little more work to be done in this area but we had done enough for one evening, hehe.

The day after, Debbie and Gina conducted a 'healing' on me, using almost every spiritual 'tool' available to them, it was that powerful.

The trapped soul from the circle had connected with me during the SR as I understand he was part of my soul's past life here!

Again, he didn't want to go, but when you have two 'Goddess' warriors working on you there is only one winner, or in this case two!

So ended this part of the SR.

'Black Magic' Circle, 2nd Visit ~ 28th July 2019

THIS VISIT WAS a short one and done in daylight, phew!

A visit to prepare the area for a visit later in the year!

Only now, having done four visits in total, did I realise the souls who remained here were very timid, fearful and reticent, as you can imagine, being the sacrificial offerings for these dark rituals.

I had to put a lot of groundwork in to gain their trust.

This visit began as I extended the existing circle by making a much larger Circle of Light before stepping into it.

Again, I forgot to ask for protection, but thankfully, it wasn't too bad; I was able to cleanse myself after by having a walk!

If a SR occurred it was a very subtle one. I felt no connection but that doesn't mean a SR hadn't taken place.

'Black Magic' Circle, 3rd Visit ~ 16th September 2019

As I WALKED around this whole area again as in visit two, I found many white feathers, eighteen in total, all in pristine condition as though they had just fallen to earth.

I took the feathers gifted to me as a sign: one feather = one soul!

I did the SR in the centre of the circle, even though the feathers were quite widespread, placing the feathers in a pile in the centre of the circle as a memorial to those who experienced the unpleasantness within this circle.

Having completed this part of the SR, I was guided about fifty yards away to a slightly denser area of trees. Three trees had a circular bank of earth formed around part of it, as if enclosing it.

I entered the circle and walked towards a cluster of three trees, one large and two smaller ones.

I walked towards the two smaller trees then stopped and faced the largest tree. I felt a connection, a soul.

To confirm this, I walked away from the spot, stopped, turned around and walked back to the same spot, again feeling the connection with this soul. I felt I needed to talk to this soul, feeling he was very wary of who I was and what I was doing there.

After ten, maybe fifteen minutes of talking to this young man, I thought he had heard enough to trust me, so I made my way back to the car and home, thinking I had done what was necessary – ending visit three perfectly, feeling I had done everything needed to complete this area's cleansing.

'Black Magic' Circle, Final Visit ~ 31st October 2019–22nd November 2019

YESTERDAY I WENT for a walk around Rivington and was guided to the same area where I have previously done SR work.

However, this visit would bring a magical end to this SR gifting me invaluable experience in the process.

I was guided to visit the area where I thought I had connected with the young man last time. Approaching the trees in the same direction, I felt the energies of a soul; it was the young man!

I was quite surprised, but also felt very emotional, to the point of crying. This was the young man's soul showing me the emotions his physical body had experienced on passing.

This is what I had connected with last time; the feelings up to and at the time of death, feeling vulnerable, fearful and very wary indeed. I feel betrayal was pivotal, leading to his demise; he was given false information to follow the adults here!

It has taken six weeks or so for this soul to trust me.

My energies and angelic friends have in some way

built up in this area enough, so that the young man could come to trust me on my return. This explains why I was talking to him for a spell and walking around the trees before leaving the last time, leaving an essence of my energies, my light.

This time, the connection was made very quickly and strongly, the young man now ready to go home, to move on. The young man/soul, was a part of my existing soul; the first connection was made so I could feel, experience and release these emotions before the last part of his journey was able to be completed!

During this last visit, I thought I had left someone behind, fear came up, only momentarily but again it's another priceless lesson.

I must trust I will always be guided to the right places, to help those souls I have an agreement with to help them return to the light ... returning as many times as is necessary, until every soul has been helped to move on, phew! This fear is another feeling stemming from the young man's soul, fear of being left behind.

22nd November 2019:
Further confirmation came via Yvonne and a message she sent me after listening to an interview I had with a lady in the USA...

The young man had actually been used in ritual sacrifice, hence my need to gain his trust; this was further confirmation I had done all that was needed.

28th November 2019:
I received some added information regarding 'our' first visit. This is a perfect example of how I gain more

knowledge about SRs the more I do; amazing!

It transpires that on this first visit 'we', Gina and I, were to focus solely on clearing the dense residual negativity, which was still present hundreds of years from when these abhorrent actions had taken place. The perpetrators will have built up this negative energy force over time and it will have gained in power the more ritual sacrifices took place.

Just as we who are 'light workers' build up our energies in our own sacred space in a positive way, the more we nurture our space, the stronger the energies become, so too with the negative energies.

As I have come to understand, trapped souls become anchored in the illusion which rendered them trapped in the first place, so, if the negativity from those who perpetrated these acts is still there, then it makes sense that those sacrificed souls aren't going to step forward to be helped until such times as the negativity is cleared.

Simply because the fearful feelings/emotions they were engulfed in during the ritual and at the time of death they may well feel it is going to happen all over again, such is the reality of the illusion they are trapped in, whether it be related to this SR or indeed any SR for that matter.

Now having cleared the negativity on this first visit, I was then able, when the time was right, to return and finish off this amazing SR.

WOW!

As of the 26th June 2020:

I now realise why, in part, it took me four visits to help this specific soul to move on. The simple answer being:

I was focusing on bringing the soul home with me, rather than focusing on doing the SR there and then. The soul will undoubtedly have moved on with my intention to help in this way.

All part of my learning curve!

'Death or Death, You Choose'
SR ~ 29th November 2018

I ADD THIS piece having just moved into a temporary home near Bolton in Lancashire.

Since moving in, I have been inundated with opportunities to let go of the deepest, darkest fears I have ever experienced, and that is saying something hehe!

A gentleman, who lives in the other room, will remain nameless but he, during our first chat, told me about the woods just at the back of the house and how he felt something while there.

During our chat, so much fear surfaced for me; it was quite uncomfortable for me at times to stay and chat, but I managed to, thankfully! Having ended this strange conversation, I came to bed with the thought that I need to visit these woods.

As midday broke the next day, I headed for the woods, only to arrive at a small wooden step which led into a field.

I stopped for a moment then suddenly froze with fear. I have never experienced anything like it.

It took me two, maybe three minutes to force myself

to overcome this hurdle and get into those woods.

On entering the woods, I felt various energies around me straight away, these were nature angels, fairies and such; so, nothing fearful thus far! It only took me a matter of five minutes to walk to the other end of the woods but as I turned to come back, I walked towards a tree, and the closer I got, the tighter my throat went.

Hmmm strange, I thought, so I stepped back a few feet then proceeded to walk towards the same tree, with the same effect.

I then knew this to be the place where the 'deed' had been done. I was shown that my soul had been hanged here in a past life. He was actually forced to hang himself, by the soul of the man in the next room and his friend!

Had I tried to explain to them this experience, it may well have caused them to feel guilty, etc., when in truth they have no need to know anything about it.

The fear multiplied the closer my soul got to the tree, for the fear to be strong at this particular point (the wooden step) must have been where my soul was able to halt the progress of those who were intent on doing this deadly deed. Even if it was just for a few minutes, it would be enough for an essence of fear to build up!

Hence why, I/Jeffrey, felt it stronger at the step than anywhere else along the path.

Anyway, back to the SR itself...

I did what I normally do at these times, I spoke kindly to all the souls trapped here, mine included, coaxing them to forgive themselves and others for what and how things had happened and to invite my SR teammates help them move on. I felt better having come to the woods; still something was amiss though, but what?

The initial frozen state I had experienced was my soul's knowing, via a stored memory, what had happened in these woods.

My soul/Shanti experienced it but to release it, I/Jeffrey, had to feel the fear such as it was, to know what I was releasing. I didn't understand this until a day or two later when I eventually calmed down and returned to normal.

Threatened No more ~ 20th April 2020
(Conclusion of the 'Death or Death, You Choose' SR)

I AGAIN VISIT the woods after having sensed over the last few days I needed to, that something was still lurking there and needed attention!

I walked straight to the tree, this time no freezing at the wooden step!

I did ask Archangel Michael and my SR friends to create a portal of light because I felt there were souls trapped there that maybe weren't ready to go the last time I visited.

Anyway, this done, I circled the tree from my last visit, feeling only a slight energy, so I placed some symbols I use to help clear the area and then I left the rest to my SR friends. From the tree I walked a little further then retraced my steps back into the woods, asking that the portal be closed as and when it was suitable.

SR completed.

I then finished my walk, coming back intending to write this piece down right away but not before I did a little relaxed meditation in the car. During this quiet time, I was gifted the reason why I needed to return to the scene of the crime, so to speak.

It involves the issue of feeling/being threatened directly, as in this SR, or indirectly in many other ways.

This was the perfect SR to use as an example.

I have said my soul was forced to hang himself, the other option was that those who were forcing me, would have killed me anyway.

A definite no win situation.

This created so much fear and confusion being pressured to do something like that, obviously the person my soul was residing in at the time caved in and took the first option!

This is a much wider issue for me but this SR has helped me see the bigger picture.

I can now work on healing and letting go of all the other times throughout my soul's journey and Jeffrey's journey in this one, all fear of being threatened.

It is surprising what can be unearthed during a SR, especially if your soul is one of the main 'actors'/'actresses' involved!

However, all this additional information, while it may seem on the surface to have little to do with any SR, is vital for your wellbeing in general to embrace any information which comes from them, to help you as it has done for me, to clear out 'our' negative baggage!

A 'Witchy' Day Indeed! ~ 1st April 2019

THIS DAY BELONGED to Debbie, my dearest friend.

I was going to Gargrave near Skipton to pick up some Hopi ear candles. When hearing about my trip, Debbie asked if she could come along. I said yes, so off we went.

As we passed through Colne, Debbie said she would like to explore the area where the Pendle Witches gained notoriety! I agreed but was a little concerned; something Debbie had said brought up some issue within me, something unpleasant.

Having done my errand, we then headed to Barrowford near Burnley, which housed the heritage centre for the Pendle Witches!

This was the start of our adventure, although nothing of note happened here, apart from a nice cup of coffee and being given a map of the area, a trail for the witches.

We headed for Roughlee, a village a couple of miles from the heritage centre. This was the birthplace of one of the women found guilty at Lancaster Castle for being a witch.

Alice was the lady's name and she also had a soul connection with Debbie. What I mean is that Debbie's soul in this present life lived in the physical body of Alice in this past life. In the village there is a statue dedicated to Alice, not in a 'witchy' guise but as the beautiful soul she was and always will be.

Her hands were bound in chains and someone had placed daffodils in the links of the chain as a mark of remembrance and/or respect, but one of the daffodils had fallen onto the floor.

Debbie approached the statue but I had stepped back, giving Debbie a quiet moment to be at one with the soul of Alice. Debbie picked the daffodil up off the floor and inserted it in one of the chain links.

At the same moment as Debbie placed the daffodil in the chain, I went tingly all over. I said, 'Is that you, Alice?' For a second nothing happened, then I felt a stronger tingling sensation all over, signalling to me this was indeed Alice!

Watching Debbie stand at the statue, and then placing the daffodil back in the chain, it was so profound and emotive, because Debbie's actions in my humble view had set Alice free from the chains in a symbolic way.

I felt so very privileged to witness this beautiful connection.

When I explained to Debbie what I saw and felt, I again went very tingly all over; again, Alice making herself clearly present. When I say Alice, I do mean that part of Alice's soul which returned here after being hanged in Lancaster.

When souls are ready to move on they use us as vehicles, to get from one place to another, seeming to know how to get to a specific place, to connect with someone who can help set the souls free. For example, me, but there are others who do this type of work as well.

Having finished what Debbie had come here to do in Roughlee, we then set off to Newchurch-in-Pendle, again just a few miles away, where Alice's family members were buried.

At the time, when being found guilty of witchcraft, the bodies were unable to be buried on consecrated ground. I was told by a lady in the village that the family was quite wealthy and her body may well have been interred with the other family members; the romantic in me hopes this is the way it was!

We went into the churchyard in Newchurch, where I set about doing soul reconnection, Alice's and other family members' souls which were also awaiting my arrival. When the reconnection had been done, I did my routine and called in my angelic friends to open a portal for the souls of Alice's family and any other souls who were in the churchyard at the time.

They all moved on swiftly, together!

However I would find out at a later visit this wasn't strictly true!

Now, a few days prior to this trip, I had a dream which gifted me the numbers 1336; this was all I remembered!

In the churchyard there was a clock on the side of the church! When I had finished the soul retrieval, I happened to look up at the clock and had it been a digital clock it would have read 13:36!

This blew me away; this was my confirmation that everything Debbie and I had done throughout the day to bring peace to these souls had been completed.

To further confirm we had completed our mission, a

friend of ours was teaching at a school in the Bolton area the same day. When I next saw her, we chatted about the experiences Debbie and I had shared in Pendle. I asked her if she had felt anything during that day.

Our friend said she felt something lift from her crown. I asked what sort of time and she said it was between 1:30 to 1:45... dare I say it – amazing!

A 'Witchy' Day: Part 2 ~ 28th July 2019

A FEW MONTHS after our first visit, Debbie and I return to a misty Pendle, taking in a Mind, Body, Spirit (MBS) show in Barley just a few miles from Newchurch, the scene of the SR on our first visit.

I felt somewhere during our short stay Debbie did indeed connect with a part of her soul from the past but not sure when and where in the village exactly. Debbie's soul having successfully connected with her then proceeded to attached itself to me, knowing I would be going back to the churchyard shortly.

This part of Debbie's soul, Alice Nutter, had stayed with Debbie after our first visit, only making herself known again when arriving here for the second time, as if she was guiding Debbie to where she needed to go, before being able to move on a little later when we revisited the churchyard in Newchurch.

Rather than a whole family SR on the first visit, I now feel we were again preparing for the finale when we returned this time.

While in Barley, we went into the village hall, seeing what the MBS show had to offer, and then went for something to eat, rounding things off with a little walk around the delightful village.

During the walk I connected to another soul as I crossed a small bridge; I sensed this soul passed in unpleasant circumstances! Having arrived back at the car, I felt the need to revisit the churchyard in Newchurch.

On my first visit, I was unable to find the gravestone where some of the Nutter family resided but this time I did.

I stood by the gravestone, feeling Debbie's soul, Alice, now finally reuniting with the souls of her family members who had been waiting for her return, so they could finally all move on together, beautiful.

As I stood there conducting the SR, I felt a searing pain just behind my left ear, only for a few seconds then it went as swiftly as it appeared. I stood by the grave for around five minutes then brought the SR to a close.

As I left the Churchyard, facing me as I closed the gate was a car with the registration plate partially showing me XXX. This I took as confirmation that today's SR had also been brought to a successful end.

Since this visit, I have been made aware the soul I connected with on the bridge was a part of my soul which had attempted to 'call' Debbie's soul's bluff by going through a mock hanging that went totally wrong!

This was a different lifetime and a different SR altogether but from the same place.

'Hanging' in Barrow Bridge ~ Thursday 30th May 2019

THE SR IN Barrow Bridge involved a friend of Mark, Janet's husband, whose name was Shaun.

He had parked his car up near Janet's house, gone into the woods and hanged himself.

He was obviously in a very dark place to have done something as drastic as this but part of his soul wasn't ready to move on, hence it became trapped.

Shortly after this happened, Shaun's wife and Janet's husband Mark went to see where Shaun did the deed, so to speak. I feel this was where Shaun's soul attached itself to Mark; they were very close friends so this is understandable.

I do feel that even though a soul becomes trapped it still has some sort of spiritual radar which helps it connect with a familiar soul in a physical body; the soul will be part of their soul group, hence the familiar feeling.

I did a healing on Mark on the 30th May and then went for a walk with Janet. It had been raining and I only had trainers on and ended up slipping, ending up quite muddied, so much so, that Janet offered to wash my jeans before I headed home.

Quite a comedy of errors, but how the angelic realm works – had I not fallen, had Janet not offered to wash my clothes, I wouldn't have had the time to connect with Shaun's soul.

Shaun needed to be able to trust me; this was part of the reason he committed suicide (trust issues) but needed to be sure he could trust me. Hence the few hours I spent with Janet and Mark waiting for my jeans to be washed was enough time for his soul to sense he could trust me.

I didn't connect with Shaun's soul until the early hours of the next morning, when I heard a bang. I just turned over and went back to sleep but as with any soul they are very persistent when they are ready to move on so I wasn't surprised when a louder bang occurred minutes later.

I woke, very groggily but as I lay there, I automatically said, 'Is that you, Shaun?' I went very cold and tingly very quickly, a sure sign it was him.

Knowing this was Shaun, I started to talk to him, preparing him for the portal to open.

When I talk to the soul(s) I do it with respect and compassion, for they are almost always in a state of confusion, not really knowing where they are or what's happened to them, so I aim to be gentle and speak in a loving caring manner. Placing them in a relaxed state, ready for their final step to move on with help from my SR friends!

When I woke in the morning, I asked had Shaun returned home and got an unequivocal 'Yes'.

Another successful retrieval had been concluded, now onto the next one!

Mother and Daughter Reunion
~ Friday 31st May 2019

BETHANY, THE DAUGHTER of another friend – another Debby – had started to hear noises and hearing a voice. She had decided to sleep downstairs because of the effect this soul had on her, it was obviously scaring her somewhat!

Debby told her daughter she had met me and that I could help with this soul if she wanted; her daughter agreed to see me. I went down on the Friday morning and had a chat with Bethany, sharing my knowledge with her about souls and how they can become trapped.

It feels unnerving more than anything else, the fact that someone other than a human is trying to contact us, albeit from beyond the grave, so to speak.

After the chat with Bethany, she led me upstairs to her room and promptly left me to connect with the soul. I spoke to the soul but invited her to come with me, rather than do the retrieval there and then for some reason; this became evidently clearer when I got home.

Back at home, I did a meditation to ground myself then started to make some tea, and during this period I felt a very powerful surge of energy all over me, very cool as well.

Again instinctively, I began to feel another presence, other than the one I thought I had connected with at Debby's.

I was then taken back to Debby's being reminded when I started to go up the stairs, I felt two subtle energies very close together; obviously I thought I had connected with just one soul but I had connected to two!

A young girl and her mother...

It transpires the young girl and the mother passed at different times, the young girl passing first at a very young age. The mother, one can only guess, couldn't cope with the loss and caused herself harm, the result being she passed in the house.

Two souls in the house each trapped, and to make it worse they were looking for each other not knowing the other soul was there, so close yet so far away! Unable to make the connection, because the two souls passed at different times in the past, which meant two different realities!

When I realised I had connected with the mother and young girl, I started to feel their energies around me. It was such a beautiful feeling and experience, to have played a part in bringing these two lost souls back together and being chosen to help set them free was very humbling indeed.

In fact, I felt the love between them so amazing that I found it hard to actually bring myself to do the retrieval.

Finally, I did, and completed the SR in the evening; a truly wonderful experience.

Bethany did return to sleep in her room just days after.

Some may question why Bethany couldn't sleep in her room with this soul being there but this 'soul experience' had triggered something within Bethany from a past life, bringing up such fear. When this happens, the fear seems so very real, I have experienced this so many times, so I say this:

Well done, Bethany, you have done incredibly well to conquer this fear!

The day after I contacted Debby and asked how things were. Debby just said the atmosphere seems peaceful.

This was my confirmation.

I had again fulfilled my role as conduit for heaven and earth to connect through me. And what a truly remarkable experience, thank you angels!

PS:

This additional information made itself known to me on the 1st October 2019:

Regarding the above SR, the two souls who were trapped, were connected to Debby and Bethany from a past life they had both experienced together. So somewhere during this present lifetime, Debby and Bethany have visited the place where this lifetime occurred.

While there, one of the trapped souls attached itself to Debby, the other attached itself to Bethany.

Again, it's nothing to be fearful of, because until you attain a level of sensitivity, able to feel or see souls, you won't know what has happened.

Both in this present lifetime and the past life, Debby's soul played the Mother and Bethany's soul was the daughter.

Initially, I thought the two souls had been trapped in Debby's current home but with the additional information I now understand this not to be the case.

Again, all a priceless learning curve for me, thank you angels!

The 'Bee' SR ~ 2nd July 2019

THIS OCCURRED AT Rivington Pike while out on a walk.

I had visited a few of my friends (various trees) and kept getting the urge to go to the village green tea room for some reason.

So off I went, walking towards the tea room, when I came across a bee on the ground. There was very little sign of movement and when nudging it very gently, I knew it had passed.

If only I had passed by earlier was my first thought but my angelic friends said, 'Every soul leaves this plain at the perfect time,' and this was such a time.

After this message I was blessed with another thought: *perhaps I was passing by, to do a SR for the beautiful bee*.

Again, I went very tingly all over, a sign I was on the right track, so to speak. The retrieval took a matter of minutes, very swift indeed! I sent love, healing and comfort to the family this bee had left behind, before inviting Archangel Michael and team to help this angel move on.

What I gained from this wonderful experience was thus:

It's wonderful doing the big retrieval experiences, such as a battlefield, etc., however, a retrieval for a single soul like the beautiful bee is just as important as any other. When I understood this insight, I felt very honoured to be gifted these opportunities to do God's work, realising if I hadn't passed by no one else would have done this retrieval!

Each SR is so unique and priceless, gifting me different experiences and a wealth of knowledge, which I can then collate and use in the future as I do more retrievals, and knowing that no one retrieval will be like any other is an added blessing!

RMS Titanic Revisited ~ 7th July 2019

SHANTI, THE NAME of my soul, has had many lifetimes, residing within many various types of bodies (man, woman, animal, etc.) experiencing many varied emotions, both happy and sad.

This latest visit to *RMS Titanic* was to set a part of Shanti's soul free!

This is another way Shanti and Jeffrey (me) combine to do SR.

I can either be asleep or in this case in a deep meditative state while doing some Reiki healing on myself, while Shanti goes off to wherever the souls are trapped in conjunction with other amazing angels, creating magical ways for the souls to move on.

Shanti 'travelled' to *RMS Titanic* a few years ago (using this method) when realising a part of his then father's soul went down with the ship, leaving part of his soul trapped in 'Davy Jones's Locker'.

Shanti ~ in that lifetime was a child.

My father's soul ~ in that lifetime was Shanti's father.

My mother's soul ~ in that lifetime was Shanti's mother.

So, just like this present life but in different bodies, experiencing different experiences in a different part of the world.

This particular SR was successful but not until this morning (7th July) did I realise that a part of Shanti's soul was still trapped there, having attached to his father's soul; the way he lost his father was very distressing and he hadn't wanted to let go!

This is one of many ways we can attach a part of our soul to loved ones or close friends, pets, etc., especially when experiencing loss in shocking, unexpected or sudden ways.

It's almost like we're not prepared to let go simply because of our strong connection through love, but when we realise and more so believe we can never lose anyone or anything, we can then begin to accept and heal the past emotions created by loss.

Arriving at a time and place in the future, when someone or something we love leaves physically or spiritually, we can accept it and carry on with our journey knowing all is well.

So, during the self-healing, Shanti went on a journey to reconnect with the part of his soul and I (Jeffrey) was blessed with a visual of what Shanti did while at *RMS Titanic*...

Shanti placed a ring of light around the whole perimeter of the wreckage and then continued to form a spiral of light upwards from the sea bed to the surface so that a portal of light, created by Archangel Michael, was able to connect with Shanti's created portal, thus allowing all souls (including Shanti's) who were ready to move on to drift effortlessly up into this beautiful light!

What a truly remarkable experience to witness via my soul.

This is why I *love* doing SR!

I cannot express fully through words how it makes me feel; the joy and love in my heart knows no bounds when playing my part in helping my brothers and sisters to move on, return to the light, to heaven or wherever you believe we go to when leaving Earth!

I am *so* blessed and honoured to be of service in this way, thank you all!

A Timely Reminder ~ 11th July 2019

A SHORT BUT very timely reminder for me to do the necessary preparation before doing any soul retrieval, after all I have been doing this for over two years now!

I was up at Rivington Pike near my home. I felt drawn to go down a dirt track which I hadn't seen before. Before I continued though, I asked my guides for protection. A strange request, as I have never done this in all my time doing SR.

I have always been too giddy (excited) to even think of protecting myself and have, on reflection, taken on 'energies' which were, shall I say unhealthy.

I do need to protect myself when doing any sort of SR because taking on any unnecessary negative energies would only affect my recovery time. While I love doing SR, and I do mean love, it can take it out of me physically and if, as is usually the case, each SR is connected to my soul's past, then it can affect my emotional and mental state, too.

So, having been gifted this timely reminder, I know it will save me a lot of heartache in the future!

Having asked for the protection I ventured down

the path very quickly, feeling my throat and stomach tighten, a sign there was some SR for my soul as well as the few others there.

I circled around a few bushes before asking Archangel Michael and other friends to bring down the portal of light for the evacuation of the remaining souls here.

This was done and dusted in a matter of minutes, leaving me feeling quite refreshed.

It was by no means a massive SR but I certainly felt the difference by using the protection on offer, helping me do the SR with more ease, which can only be good news for me!

Lesson learned!

Mum and Dad SR ~
1st August 2019

I WAS WATCHING the film *The Shack* again last night, when a scene initiated a thought: *I may need to do some more SR for Mum and Dad*.

I have done this on a few occasions for Mum since she passed in 2005 and for Dad when he passed in 2016. Each time it hurt so much to do but it was necessary, otherwise I would have left well alone. (I have added a SR regarding Dad in the earlier pages of this book.)

The difference with this SR, I was ready to let go. The other times, I was letting go bit by bit; as much as I could cope with!

So, as the film came to an end, I felt Mum but more so Dad with me. I then began the SR. It was a simple one to do, simply because I knew the history. I didn't need to do research to see what resonated with me as I do with most of the other SRs.

Like I said, the key to this successful completion of Mum and Dad's moving on was the fact that I was *ready* for them to move on and I was ready to move on, too!

In truth, all I was doing was letting go of the unhealthy parts I had held on to of Mum and Dad.

I add this SR because when the time comes for you to let go of your loved ones, hopefully you will take solace from my words, helping you realise that doing this is hard but it's a necessary part of the healing process and a priceless gift you can give to those you are holding on to.

Setting yourself and those loved ones free; taking your relationship to a higher level of consciousness, a level where unconditional love reigns! The blessing for me having done the SR.

Throughout the day after, I slowly began to feel a large weight had been lifted off my shoulders, the day simply just got better and better, and long may it continue!

Rivington 'Clean-up' Done ~ 8th August 2019

YESTERDAY, WHILE ON my way up to Rivington, I felt I was to do some SR, tying up loose ends if you will.

As I walked, I found my path would cover both the dark areas in which I have done a lot of SR work and also the village area, bringing the two areas together energetically.

It was raining; I believe rain to be a sign of a cleansing going on, be it for mother earth or indirectly for all within the perimeter of the rainfall, whether they are aware of it or not!

I stopped at the same point where I had previously visited, doing black magic SRs on each occasion.

I feel this was to allow added information to come to me regarding this area.

I returned home and thought nothing about it until I was rudely awakened by a rattling noise, but as soon as I sat up the noise stopped, signalling something was about to show itself.

I went very tingly and cold; a sign a soul was with me.

I asked questions which came to me during this conversation, leading me to believe this spirit was a part of my soul, Shanti, and that I had connected to it on my second visit.

So, as I do, rolled my sleeves up, called on my SR friends and within minutes this trapped soul had moved on. Happy days!

Ease Our Pain (Dad's and Mine)
~ 14th August 2019

THE PREVIOUS FORTY-EIGHT hours I had been seeing lots of physical and psychic signs regarding Dad. I didn't realise what they meant until I woke up in the early hours, after a very vivid 'dream experience'.

I had been shown a past life with Dad.

The lifetime in question was in the North of England in the 30s; this is the era I kept getting so I must trust it! I saw Dad and myself standing in what seemed to be a hotel foyer.

It was a very emotional scene!

Dad was leaving but didn't want to go. I didn't want Dad to go either but he had no choice. The last vision I received was of Dad and me hugging passionately, tears flowing from both of us. I sense Dad was leaving for health reasons amongst other issues, and I also felt I would never see him again!

The main feeling from this scene was the pain I felt regarding Dad leaving. I felt I was losing him all over again; the pain was too much to bear.

Both an essence of Dad's and my emotional memory had built-up in this hotel; it was the last time 'they' would see each other, so, from this emotional scene our memories had soaked into the walls, etc. of the hotel.

The dream experience ends.

Having woken up, feeling these raw emotions, tears flowed physically, fast and hard. I calmed down and now, in a semi-meditative state, I was shown this was an EC urgently needing to be dealt with. The EC had already occurred during the dream experience but I had to feel the pain from it.

I (Jeffrey) needed to play my part by releasing this pain through my physical body.

It brought an end to our karmic relationship regarding the issue of loss, and indeed balanced all karma between Dad's soul and mine, yay!

The final vision I received while in this meditative state was amazing. The essences of Dad and myself from this lifetime were being symbolically escorted back to the light or heaven, hand in hand, walking home together, beautiful!

This was our angelic friend's way of showing me the EC had been completed, it was very gratefully received, thank you angels!

Again, it was another example of how we really have no idea what excess baggage we are carrying from other lifetimes, unknown quantities of negative feelings/emotions which affect our 'now' life.

However, through SR in various forms we are now able release this unnecessary weight from our shoulders, yay!

'Dad Had To "Let Go Too"' SR ~ 23rd September 2019

TODAY I HAVE been to see *Aladdin*, again (third time in a week, I really enjoy it) and have been gifted more insight as to a little bit of SR to finish off the attachment between Dad and me.

Throughout all the SRs I have done to let go of Dad; none have actually worked on his attachment to me; this is what I was shown in the film.

Again, it's something which never crossed my mind but has surfaced at the perfect time for us to fully let go from both sides.

Driving to the cinema, I saw a van with the word 'lineage' all over it; a definite sign but I had no idea what part of my lineage until I watched the film. And the song 'No More "I Love You's"' by Annie Lennox was playing on the radio just before I arrived at the cinema.

On my short journey home after the film, the song 'Ain't No Stopping Us Now' by McFadden & Whitehead blasted out from the radio.

It was my angelic friend's way of saying: 'The first song relates to the past... The second is now saying both you and your dad are free to move on in a very positive sense.'

As the song title suggests, ain't no stopping either me or Dad now; fantastic, so happy for Dad as much as for myself!

There is however a little SR to be done but I feel this will be the easiest one I have done for either of my parents from this lifetime especially!

Dad has had the fear that something unpleasant would happen to me, he has been protective of me in this lifetime but he chose control as his way of protection. Alas, all his attempts at control have had no success for I have experienced everything I have needed to regardless:

On a physical level for Jeffrey and my ancestral Lineage!

And on a spiritual level for Shanti!

This is what Dad has needed to let go of at this time, the perfect time as I step up my SR work out in the field, so to speak.

Thank you, Dad, for your help in all ways. Love you!

Landlady and Her 'Ex' ~ 14th September 2019

THIS BEGAN ON the morning of the 14th September, around 2.30am.

My landlady, Dee, (an alias) had an unpleasant dream experience, ending in Dee releasing a loud shriek, purely because the experience seemed so real! The noise from downstairs woke me up; it had to be loud enough, so I would go and see what the matter was.

Now downstairs, Dee said she had had a very vivid dream of her ex being here, holding her down by her arms and finally telling her he was going upstairs to rest. She was quite shaken as I started to piece this situation together.

I did feel a presence in my room on waking but thought nothing of until I got downstairs. We chatted a while and it soon became clear to me that the soul of Dee's ex was here, simply seeking to move on. He sought forgiveness from Dee's soul in this specific past life and perhaps this present one too; unable to move on until Dee forgave him and let him go for both their sakes!

Dee thought he was here for other things, causing her

to become fearful.

During our chat, Dee said she and her ex used to travel around Yorkshire quite lot when they were together as an item, so to speak! Instantly I felt that during one of these trips they had visited a specific place where they had experienced a past life, an unpleasant one, and had connected to their own specific essences or souls from this life until a time they could bring this to a peaceful conclusion ... which happened to be this morning!

I told Dee I would go to bed and do a SR to help both souls forgive and let go.

Alas, both ways I have been guided to help souls return home didn't work! The talking and inviting them to step into the light and then having asked my angelic friends to oversee this completion during dreamtime, nothing happened or so I thought!

Later that same day I was guided into nature up to Rivington near my home. I was taken to a tree I had recently connected with, a beautiful sycamore tree. As I approached the tree, I remembered how its energies felt when first we met; the energies around the area felt very heavy. I thought nothing of this at the time; I just spent a little time with the tree enjoying the energies then continued my walk.

The scene was now set!

After this morning's events, I was now standing beside the tree, feeling the need to walk around the area, creating a Circle of Light with my angelic friends' help. I did this, which was quite treacherous at times, very muddy!

Having completed the circle, all the while talking to other souls who were within this circle to ready themselves, if they chose, to move-on via a portal of light created by my walk and Archangel Michael and team of light-working angels!

This included Dee's and her ex's souls, too. The more SRs I do the more my spiritual vision becomes clearer. I felt drawn to go into the bushes to coax out what I sensed to be a little girl (Dee's soul) feeling emotional as I did so.

She was very wary of me but when an adult soul approached her, she took his hand and came from the bushes; only now do I feel this was Dee's ex.

I saw two figures, two simply rounded forms, cloaked in a green hue walking from the bushes, but boy was that enough; I was blown away with this vision.

They walked into the portal of light hand-in-hand, a sign, all had been forgiven!

A wonderful feeling, again knowing I had done all that was asked of me and more importantly the forgiving had taken place!

'Comfort Blanket' SR ~ 27th September 2019

I FELT IT necessary to call upon my ancestors to help heal and bring completion to an ongoing issue; some of my ancestors were involved, even those who still reside here on earth in a physical presence!

I had a dream experience which showed me travelling on a coach, where it was heading to, I have no idea but the coach had all the main protagonists of my life in Leigh.

At one point I said something like, 'Enough is enough,' and got off the coach.

Basically, I have used this part of my life in Leigh as a comfort blanket and needed, for my sake, to break free of the cords and attachments which held me there. I wasn't ready to do this until I woke, understanding the vision I had been gifted. I was emotional when waking from the dream experience; even though those times crucified me and by my own sword, as it were, I found it hard to let go and to my surprise, I was the one holding on!

This, however, was the perfect opportunity to do so; a SR was needed.

This was done before I went back to sleep, asking that all parts/cords and attachments be severed for the highest will and good for all concerned. My actions have again set myself free from these no longer needed attachments and also set those souls free who played a large part of my time in Leigh.

This SR was again slightly different for I feel there was a gathering somewhere in heaven, if you wish, a place of neutrality, bringing each soul together to iron out any misunderstandings, to allow offerings of forgiveness and thanks from myself and any other soul who felt it necessary to balance the karma between my soul and theirs.

Unless the souls of the other 'people' at this gathering have some semblance of spiritual awareness, they will have no idea about what went on.

They will benefit from this coming together but have no need to know what went on because it could easily cause them to feel an array of negative emotions; there is no need to do this, especially if they aren't ready to understand, accept and release on a conscious level.

This was obviously successful as on waking I felt a weight had lifted from my shoulders; thankfully, I had the support in spirit to attain this – thank you, angels!

I do thank every soul who played a part in my torrid but necessary life in Leigh, without going through those experiences I wouldn't be where I am now, so again: Thank you!

Personal SR ~ 29th September 2019

I AGAIN HAD a dream experience which instigated a truly amazing cleansing for me, involving a SR for parts of my soul.

The dream experience:
I was in someone's house looking down the side of a settee/couch for any coins which may have fallen out of the pocket of an unsuspecting visitor/resident. It would only have amounted to pence rather than pounds but I was very thorough in my search.

At this point Mum made her entrance. My actions brought up such shame and embarrassment, that I couldn't look her in the eye.

I woke quite emotional, but it did give me the impetus to seek further information regarding this issue which has plagued me all my life and back through many lifetimes, as I have found out during past healings, etc. The lack and loss of money!

This time I was taken back to a lifetime in Persia via the film *Aladdin*:

My soul was a child living on the street with no parents

and very little food, etc. I begged and stole food and other items I needed. I soon became known as a thief to the locals and treated as you could imagine, not very nicely! I was told many times I was worthless, useless and other more colourful language, all of which heaped such a lack of self-worth upon my young shoulders.

Now, there are other lifetimes this worthlessness issue has played out, so the SR I was guided to do was again to be done while I/Jeffrey slept.

My soul and all those who played roles in my learning regarding worthlessness gathered in a neutral setting somewhere in heaven.

Again, forgiveness was the main item on the agenda, because while the initial life showed my soul as a pauper, my soul has experienced the other side of the coin too, having experienced great wealth.

Success was attained!

My next dream experience, later the same morning, showed me a vision which confirmed a healing had occurred. I had seven blisters on my right foot, in a specific formation; they then turned into blood blisters. The dream moved to a vision of my foot with a clear plaster covering the entirety of my foot. The plaster was removed, allowing a large amount of fluid to be released. The emotions, having built up and then burst, allowed the physical release to take place.

I woke up with my right foot tingling greatly; this signifying the release had brought about an ease in movement. I am now able to move forward with more ease on my soul's journey without this worthlessness issue hanging over me like a guillotine waiting to drop at any moment.

Now all this having come to an end, I looked at the time, it was: 5.55am – a definite sign that a big change was imminent after the releasing done during the SR.

Wonderful!

Money, Betrayal and Dad ~ 2nd & 3rd Oct 2019

THIS ISSUE HAS been building up nicely over the last few days.

The evening of the 2nd of October I was blessed with a few signs showing me the issue with money and Dad had still to be fully resolved.

I had a vision of going to the bank and drawing some money out, feeling a little uncomfortable. This was after I had been ejected from my home, Dad having come at me with a knife; thankfully, it was only a superficial wound but it instigated a series of events, unpleasant to say the least.

I had to leave because the authorities deemed Dad to be *compos mentis* to live on his own with the aid of carers. It has taken a while for me to forgive those who made this decision but I have finally done so, however this left me without a home, a job and in truth a Dad, such were the after effects of Dad's actions.

(This has been written about in detail in the *Darkness Was, As Light Is Now...* book.)

At the time of the attack, Dad was recovering from a stroke which left him with very, very limited speech.

Understanding what he was trying to say was a challenge indeed, even after seven years of caring for him; only God knows how tough it was for Dad, knowing what he wanted to say but unable to relay those words, frustrating indeed!

Dad was also in the grip of fear as he was trying to control me through his actions.

This was Dad's way of trying to protect me from the unpleasant experiences of the world; this was his way of showing he loved me, bless him!

A valiant attempt to save me but as we know we are unable to save anyone but ourselves, as whatever our soul has chosen to experience, it will, regardless of any attempts from others to save us!

In addition, Dad was trying to come to terms with loss especially of loved ones, namely my brother Jack who passed over after only twenty-four hours of life, Dad's mum and dad, then his wife (my mum) and add to that the friends who seemed to abandon him throughout his life; he really had a lot to contend with while alive.

I state categorically: I have forgiven Dad for everything which occurred the moment he came at me with the knife, before and what came after. I have only the greatest of respect and love for Dad and what he experienced on his journey.

Dad did what he had to, to get me out of the house and then keep me out; his soul knew it had to do this, for my soul, residing within Jeffrey had and has a path to fulfil, where he needed time to recover from this first part of his lifetime in Leigh before continuing on his journey.

Anyway, back to the issue.

It's no surprise that it's money, again, with added feelings of betrayal on my part thrown in for good measure!

The vision of me drawing money out made me realise I had felt guilty each time, when using Dad's money to improve my health during the time of eviction, regarding somewhere to live, food, etc. I felt at a deep subconscious level I was betraying Dad but had I not used the money in the way I did I wouldn't be here now.

The morning after, I did a meditation.

A Steve Nobel one: Energetic Imprint Removal Transmission: Clearing Highly Charged Energies with A Person or Situation!

I must say Steve's transmissions have helped me a great deal over the last eighteen months...

Thank you for producing such divine meditations, Steve!

As the transmission began, I felt Dad very strongly on my right side; this continued throughout. By the end, I do believe Dad and I had come to understand both sides of this life experience, with Dad understanding what I had been through and vice versa.

This brought about a karmic balancing of all our lifetimes of experiences together.

Finally, the SR was for me to release my grip on Dad's soul, so that forgiveness was able to be offered and accepted by both Dad and myself, bringing completion to a challenging life together.

Through this series of events this was attained during the evening, with the gracious help of Archangel Michael and our angelic friends.

It was a simple SR because both Dad and my soul were ready to heal the past but the simple ones can also be the most wonderful experiences, too!

Injustice ~ 4th & 5th Oct 2019

This hidden issue was instigated by words from my dear friend Yvonne, who did a healing on me around ten years ago.

Yvonne said something like, 'Being who you are, you won't want to pay taxes to subsidise "acts of war", etc., so may choose to live somewhere that is conducive.'

This message isn't exactly word for word, I have written it how I perceived it to be. The 'who you are' is a pointer to my soul, Shanti, being a Master of Peace!

To be honest, regardless of my soul's name or Jeffrey my Earth name, I would rather be living somewhere where any tax I pay is used on other things to help everyone, rather than on any war or type of conflict.

This is who I *am* now, having been opened up to the truth of who I *am* and who we all are!

The message served to plant a seed within my subconsciousness to awaken past-life issues where taxation of various types caused untold hardship and unpleasantness all around for the lesser well off, shall I say.

For those of a lower class were subjected to all sorts of unjust actions and laws created by royalty, governments, etc. without any support whatsoever, having their hard-earned money and material items forcibly removed, forcing them into poverty and service in one way or another for king and country, so to speak.

True, a few just men and women in each of those lifetimes stood up for the cause and rebelled.

This is where the issue has arisen for me, for my soul Shanti has obviously experienced lifetimes of rebelling, but has also experienced the other side of the coin by being co-creator of these taxes and laws to suit the few rather than the many.

It's like anything when we are the causer of any situation, especially if it involves being detrimental to others, we don't really understand what all the fuss is about. When the lower classes start to revolt, we either ignore or just become arrogant to the plight of others, when we are in a position of power we don't really care what happens.

Only when things start to get uncomfortable will we look at change and even this will include saving our own skin first and foremost!

It is only in the second phase, when our soul begins to experience the dark side of these created taxes and laws we then feel all the other emotions connected to the state of being abused, having our rights taken away with no power to do anything, etc. We feel cheated, abandoned and betrayed by our peers.

But this is how our soul's journey has always been, to experience both sides of the coin, for then we can choose our path by using these past experiences and make a decision on how to move forward in life by doing the same or using our experiences to help bring in change.

A few days prior to this issue surfacing, I watched the film *Robin Hood*, the 2018 version. Robin Hood is well-known for 'robbing the rich to pay the poor', whether truth or legend but in this version of the film Robin of Loxley was conscripted to fight for the king and during his time away fighting his entire estate was confiscated by the powers that be, adding it to their 'war chest'.

On his return home to England, seeing his home and belongings now in the hands of the sheriff, he was more than a little upset, so took it upon himself to do something about the situation.

This is where the legend comes to the fore, with Robin Hood and his band of merry men robbing the rich to pay the poor.

The film brought up deep feelings of injustice for me. It had to, to awaken these dormant feelings up for my soul, who has obviously played a part in a lifetime similar to the Robin Hood example!

While watching the film, and the days since, I have felt souls around me, souls connected to this lifetime and souls who were now ready to move on. This feeling of injustice stayed with me for a while, so I could embrace and accept the feelings, then let them go and forgive those perpetrators, forgiving myself for playing the role of one of those perpetrators in another lifetime, accepting all my soul has experienced, now able to bring this issue to an end.

Also in this issue, I have understood I need to accept that until I move to a country which doesn't provide funding for war I must accept the laws of this or any other country I live in and, more importantly, simply pay my dues as and when without any judgement and allow those involved with these laws to get on and experience their chosen path, for they too are souls on a journey.

For Jeffrey/Shanti it is to learn to love paying these dues and let go of any drama, detach and follow my soul's journey, where I am best served to help this world bring in a new era.

Again the SR is a simple one to do, for having seen this issue from all sides, making a decision to let go and move on, my soul can be at peace now.

I know this batch of experiences doesn't spend too much time on the SRs but I felt it necessary to add them to the book, giving you another example of how we can access our souls' past lives in our own way and do SRs for ourselves when having the necessary level of spiritual knowledge to do so.

Indian 'Nightmare' ~ 8th Oct 2019

TUESDAY MORNING I woke from a deep sleep, only to receive one word as a sign from this subconscious state: INDIA.

I believe a SR took place but because of the severity of my soul's experiences in this particular past life, I was spared the visual effects which were played out in this lifetime.

In the recent past, I have been gifted the story regarding this lifetime in India. My soul resided within a young child who had lost his parents and was found wandering the streets. He was taken in by people who abused his situation and violated his body, doing unpleasant things to his eyes, rendering him blind, so he would be more successful when sent out to beg!

A few years ago I saw a scene, via a film called *Slumdog Millionaire*, where children were actually experiencing what I have written in the above paragraph and how they rendered the children blind; this brought up so much emotion at the time. Obviously, I needed to be made aware of this lifetime so I was able to release these feelings.

This latest SR took us back to the scene of the crime, so to speak, to set free this part of our soul, now we have been able to release all the relevant emotions from this life and indeed others where my soul has experienced great despair, being homeless, having no family to support him, being abused, passed from pillar to post, etc.

All these experiences, lifetimes, helping to create a vast cavern of worthlessness, which again has come to the fore to finally be released through my physical body and my soul, Shanti, going to all corners of this world setting free each sliver of his soul connected to these lifetimes, culminating in the travelling back to India to bring closure to this period of Shanti's soul journey.

Again, there is very little explanation of the SR but I feel there is great learning to be shared through Shanti's many lifetimes. Sharing the lessons with you will help you if/when you come to do SR for your own soul and/or as I have done, agreed to come back in this lifetime because I had promised many other souls to return to help them move on.

I believe this is the one of the greatest honours I will ever receive, simply because I'm able to help my brothers and sisters who are trapped in limbo, trapped in an illusion which goes round and round, never stopping, until someone like myself or any other person who can do SR work to an acceptable standard helps them because these souls deserve to be treated with the utmost respect, regardless of what they have experienced or caused other souls to experience. As I have said many times now, this is our soul's journey and they experience both sides of the coin, so they can then choose how to move forward from that moment. It's all a learning, a remembering of who and what our soul is!

It's a gradual process and has to experience everything which it isn't, to realise what and who our soul truly *is*...

Wellington Bomber Crash Site, Anglezarke, 1st Visit ~ 21st August 2019 to 6th November 2019

I WENT FOR a walk around Rivington, having been told by a friend about a plane crash which happened in this area.

My friend and I had almost walked to the site the day before but turned back just yards before reaching it; obviously my friend wasn't meant to be with me while doing the SR.

Beginning the SR I started to ascend a path through some trees, which is where I connected with the first soul. At the top of the hill, stands a monument to those who died in the crash; this is where I connected with the second and most prevalent soul.

While standing at the monument, I felt an overwhelming feeling this soul had caused this crash through his actions. Whatever he did or didn't do when the plane was plunging toward the ground, he felt guilty he had let his comrades down.

Understandable but unnecessary!

This soul was part of my soul, Shanti's, history and in time I was proved right.

While stood at the monument, I saw a path leading into the distance but I didn't want to go down it; when these feelings come, I know that is just what I need to do.

Just a few hundred yards along this path I connected with another soul, which was emitting much anger, energetically. I then retraced my steps back to the monument and headed down to the stream, crossing a little bridge. Just after the bridge I connected with another soul.

A little further along I passed two men chatting. I sensed these two men were here as a conduit for their soul's retrieval; their souls were obviously connected to this crash site and the souls within it!

They would have known nothing about my work but the return of those souls connected to them would have released negative feelings they no longer needed to hold on to.

Having passed the two men, I reached the bridge I crossed signalling the start of the SR, bringing the circle to completion.

I had connected to six souls, which happened to be the same number of men killed in this crash, but there will have been other souls within this circle from times gone by who also had an opportunity to return home too.

This is why I love doing SR work. It helps so many, on many levels without me knowing about it. I am *so* blessed!

I have, in addition to the SR, been blessed through

the connection with the part of my soul from the monument, an opportunity to release, from many past-lives, the feeling of letting people down. This has been a heavy weight to subconsciously carry upon my shoulders since the original connection occurred but thankfully, this too has now been lifted.

This came to pass on the 6th November 2019.

Wellington Bomber Crash Site, Anglezarke, 2nd Visit ~ 20th January 2020

I RETURN TO Anglezarke today, the 20th of January 2020.

This came about because a part of my soul made his presence felt only last evening.

He has been with me since the first visit, for a few reasons:

He needed to attain a level of self-forgiveness.

He was also in need of courage to return to the site and face the other soul involved.

It has taken time for me to become aware of and release the emotions I/Jeffrey was to let go of on his behalf. This part had been completed; confirmed by the part of my soul contacting me in such a vivid way, energetically.

I was made aware that four souls from the crash had moved on but as you are about to read, two souls were still around: the trapped part of my soul who was with me, and the other trapped soul who was too angry to move on.

For a period before and after my first visit, I kept

receiving the word 'aneurysm' and if I'm totally honest it brought up fear in me.

I thought it was a message for me in the here and now but through last night's connection I was reassured it was the instigator of the crash for my soul who, in this past life was a sergeant, experienced a dizzy spell which led to the plane's demise.

My mind was conjuring up how today would play-out but again it was an opportunity for me to allow the powers that be to guide me without expectation, which brought about an amazing ending.

I *am* learning!

As I set off towards the area of the crash, I felt very anxious. This was my soul's past emotion surfacing, concerned how the other soul who had been part of the altercation was going to react when we arrived.

If I may go back to my first visit… While stood at the monument, I saw a path leading into the distance but I didn't want to go down it. As I have said previously, this was because it felt unpleasant in some way.

This time I had an inkling why I felt as I did, knowing the emotion I sensed was anger. The other soul was in charge of this operation, either the captain or main pilot.

My soul experienced the dizzy spell leading him to lose focus on the job at hand, which in turn obviously led to the plane crashing.

The captain in all the melee thought my soul had been incompetent in some way, so fired off a barrage of verbal abuse; quite understandable in this sort of situation.

Again, on my first visit I completed a circle as I walked across a little bridge, thus sealing the area in light. This was to help those souls who were ready to move on, as it turned out, the other four people on the plane.

Now here a second time, I was to help the two remaining souls move on but before that I was to mediate between them, to help them put their differences to bed, as it were.

One can only try to imagine, but in a situation like this there had to be a lot of chaos ensuing from my soul's initial dizzy spell through to the final act of the plane crashing. Hence the 'crossed wire' scenario!

I made my way to the same spot where the other soul was and sure enough, I felt the same presence connect with me.

I explained to the soul the events which led up to the plane crashing. After a few moments the soul finally accepted my explanation and joined me, as I set about completing the circle once again.

Only this time I came back into the circle and down a path, which led me to an old disused mine shaft.

I felt it was the perfect place to complete the SR and indeed for any other souls who were within the Circle of Light. All were blessed with an opportunity to move on.

Magical!

'Pirate of the Caribbean' ~ 10th June 2010 to 13th November 2019

THE WAY THIS came into my awareness blew me away and no mistake!

This morning I began to do some self-healing, to help release other feelings which had surfaced over the last few days, namely feeling I was always second best. (This issue has been written about in a SR previously regarding my dad and Uncle Ian!) Also, feeling I had let people down throughout many lifetimes too.

However, one issue has been so hard to completely let go of, the issue regarding money and, more importantly, the fear of losing money or material wealth when I have had it.

During the healing I fell asleep. I saw two dragonflies, that was it visually but on waking I soon began to receive information regarding this issue and the lifetime where it was at its most challenging, shall I say.

It comes from a life as a 'pirate' in and around the Caribbean. Now, I love watching the *Pirates of the Caribbean* films, yet I've never once noticed the signs within the title of the films or the films themselves, which I have watched many times over.

1. It has given me a starting point as to where the healing, acceptance and releasing needs to begin.
2. It also shows me why when setting off on my travels in June 2010 to, funnily enough, the Caribbean on a Writer's Workshop Cruise: leaving and returning to Fort Lauderdale, stopping at several destinations, including Ochos Rios in Jamaica, Cayman Islands, Cozumel and the Bahamas, fear and other emotions surfaced during this entire yet amazing trip!

As I left home on this adventure, I travelled to London, staying there overnight then caught the train to Heathrow the morning after to fly out to Miami.

I stayed in London, rather than getting a flight from Manchester simply because it was a direct flight, London to Miami, from Manchester it would have meant two flights; one flight too many, hehehe!

This short journey from my hotel to the train station was fraught with indecision; every few steps I stopped and questioned myself, *am I really doing this*? Anyone who saw me do this would have questioned my sanity, hehe!

I had, at the time, a real fear of flying, so to go to the USA on my own and without any alcohol in my system seemed quite illogical to put it mildly!

I managed to calm myself and got on the plane, again with more than a little fear surfacing when coming face to face with the door of the plane, but I forced myself on.

Once in the air I began to calm down, only to get about half-way to Miami when the plane suddenly dropped, I don't know how far but some people took in a deep gasp, as I did.

Boy, how it brought up fear though; had I been able to get off the plane I would have been a very happy chappy, hehe! I was so glad I took my crystal prayer bowl with me because for the remainder of the flight it did some hard work keeping me calm enough to cope.

So, I landed in Miami and arrived at my hotel for the night in Fort Lauderdale. Leaving my possessions in the room, I ventured across the road for some food. While waiting, I happened to look at the TV where the news headline read *Hurricane Week*.

That was enough, I said, 'I'm going home.'

However, I overcame that thought, slept quite well and arrived at the port to board the ship, named *Emerald Princess*, which stood at around eighteen levels high.

This brought up my fear of heights, only when I looked at the sheer size of the ship, which brought to mind the saying: 'It never rains, but it pours', meaning misfortunes or difficult situations tend to follow each other in rapid succession; perfect explanation of my journey, hehe!

Throughout the cruise the sea was like a mill-pond, so still.

Having now understood this past-life issue, I know these self-imposed road-blocks were challenges I needed to overcome so I could finally connect with the part of my soul trapped in Jamaica – the lifetime which best highlights the hoarding and loss of treasure, the fear of losing money or material wealth when I have had it.

It all makes so much sense now, phew!

So, all I need to do now is a SR, helping this part of my soul to move on, allowing me to finally let go of the illusion of this fear and loss. Because until I do let go completely, I will never accrue any amount of material wealth in this present lifetime without subconsciously fearing I'm going to lose it all, again!

Talk about perfect timing!

It has taken nine long years to finally bring this most challenging issue to a magical end. It's felt like forever carrying these feelings and fears around with me but they have helped me in so many wonderful ways!

The gift I've been blessed with: I now have such priceless knowledge to share with and help others going through similar issues!

'Witch Doctor/Healer' of the Caribbean ~ 10th June 2010 to 14th April 2020

THE CULMINATION OF ten years' unseen SR work was brought to an end earlier today!

The soul who woke me this morning was called Annie and was very persuasive, shall I say, about getting me to oversee this SR.

To give you a little insight:

My soul, in this past life was a healer and had told the parents of a young boy that he could save him; the boy was very poorly indeed! My soul did all he could but the boy passed, leaving the parents so distraught the mother viciously cursed the healer, my soul's body!

Annie, it turns out, was the mother of the child. I asked how did she connect with me?

I got the reply that she made her way to Martha Brae in the style of the title of this book, *Taxi for Spirit*. She was able to hitch a ride on the back of the person who now houses the remainder of Annie's soul, connecting with me at the precise location where I was to be found, when experiencing the river cruise in 2010.

So, she has been with me ever since, quietly biding her time until it was time for her and the other souls involved to be set free to move on. I spoke to her about forgiving my soul, for what he had inadvertently caused, explaining that his passion for helping sometimes overstepped the mark and that this was unfortunately one of those times.

We chatted for a quite a while; I did feel it necessary to spend time with Annie making sure everything was understood!

The simple fact she made herself known this morning was a sign she was ready to forgive. I felt the need to explain to her my soul's side of the story and that he didn't do this on purpose. And whatever she did via the curse, it was nothing compared to the self-berating my soul has done ever since that unpleasant experience.

It has been a major learning curve for me, because I have been made aware, throughout many lifetimes, where my soul has tried to overcompensate for its actions when causing other souls to experience trauma, conflict, etc.

My soul felt the need to go that extra mile while trying to save other souls, thinking he needed to do something extreme to balance his past, to regain God's favour when there has been no need!

So, the lesson for me is: rather than trying to save a soul, focus on helping them through healing, whatever the outcome.

The SR was completed as I slept and has had a positive effect on a relationship I have found hard to forgive until now.

Forgiveness for placing a curse upon my soul; this

curse has now been cleared, the others involved will, whether they feel anything or not, be able to move forward in life with a much lighter load than before this came to light!

'Stillborn' ~ 21st April 2020

I WOKE EARLY in the morning, to be shown the truth of the previous SR.

Helen, a lady I have been chatting with in Vegas, USA, her soul and her husband's soul in this present lifetime, were involved with the SR.

I now believe the child was stillborn; the soul having already merged with the baby's body. The mother was obviously going through great trauma during her pregnancy, then to have hope given to you via a doctor/healer during pregnancy must have given the couple such a boost. However, to have that joy taken away when the child was born must have been so very hard to accept.

In this alone I understood why a curse was forthcoming from the mother, understandable!

The child's soul was part of Heather's soul, a lady I have connected with in this lifetime, also living in the USA.

When I found this out it upset me greatly, simply because I know she is a very pure and loving person in this lifetime, but I must detach from this and realise our souls came together to experience a specific issue which would help finally balance the karma we have played out for however long.

Through our chat I felt the forgiveness had been

gifted to my soul, simply by the connection with Helen, which she has also benefited from by forgiving, as it sets her soul free too.

Having found out it was Heather's soul, I then needed to forgive myself that bit more because our soul connection is a very strong one. All forgiveness occurring at a higher level, no forgiveness was asked for on a physical level!

Confirmation, if I needed it, came via an A-ha song called 'Stay on These Roads'. It mentions very early on in the song 'Stillborn by choice'. Every time in the past I have listened to this song, these three words have brought up much emotion, as it did when realising who the child's soul was.

And in the video, there is a lady clearing snow from her home and it just looked like Heather; another piece of confirmation!

It also explains even further why I struggled to make my way to the USA for the cruise; I felt my soul definitely knew what was coming.

Having had this added to the other lifetime(s) in the Caribbean, no wonder I found it hard to overcome but overcome it I did, yay!

So, while I have struggled to grasp the truth in this SR, it's another priceless piece of learning.

I was going through a phase of doubting myself and asked for others advice, but while their input was pure it simply confused me more, until I was guided to relax, let go of this SR for a day or two then, when the time was right as in this morning, I received all the information I sought.

So, in a word, to me and to you: Patience!

The 'Pop-up Surprise' SR ~ 4th November 2019

TODAY WAS THE first day of a business course occurring in Bolton.

I did the full two-week course in May earlier this year but felt drawn to attend this one, too.

Things began to make sense as I arrived at the car park, where it usually cost £4 for the day. The tariffs had changed since my last visit; the cost for the day was now £10. I was unable to afford £10 but this happened for a reason as you are about to find out.

As I sat waiting for the course to begin, I started to mull over the cost of the car park and decided I would leave at the lunch interval.

It wasn't what I had planned but hey, we've got to trust our angels, haven't we?

During the three-hour stay I had come in contact with an energetically unpleasant trapped soul, having been 'chauffeured' around by a person who had no idea what was occurring, and it shall stay that way!

The person will, however, have been affected by the feelings/emotions of this soul since the time of their connection.

The person's task in this situation is to help release these feelings/emotions, because the trapped soul is a sliver of their existing soul, seeking help to move on to heal, so it can return to connect with their present soul at a later date.

All this happening without the person having any inclination of what was going on!

This is when I say to people, if you feel an emotion which is alien to you, that you have no idea where it has come from, it's a good sign you have connected to a trapped part of your own soul and have taken on the role of releaser for it.

By the time I had returned to the car, I felt absolutely drained. I headed back in the direction of home but was then guided to take a detour up to Rivington.

This is where the SR was to come to a wonderful end. The area where I was to do the SR had already been made known to me a while ago; a SR done at the time but obviously not finished!

I was left in no doubt by the soul, via a coldness and tingling all over, that we had reached the spot where the SR was to take place.

The first time I have experienced this to this degree!

My initial thought: *Why did this soul connect with the person, then connect with me, only to come back to the same spot it most certainly was connected with originally?*

Mmm, curious indeed!

The person had obviously walked past this area at some point in their life, unbeknownst to them, connecting to this sliver of their soul and at the same time taking on the emotions/feelings from this lifetime, to release and let them go; which had all been pre-agreed.

Then, and only then, would the sliver of their soul be ready to transfer from them to me. I was then able to fulfil my promise to bring about a positive outcome to this part of their journey.

The trapped soul had obviously died in tragic circumstances which, as I arrived at the place of the SR, were borne out.

Indeed, the soul was involved in a sacrificial ritual. I feel this soul was the one being sacrificed, anger being the main emotion I sensed from the soul.

However, I know anger when looked into deeply, will almost always result in the core issue being fear.

I feel the physical body of this soul was venting anger just before death, perhaps vowing revenge, for the energies I felt from this person were very sharp and bitter to say the least.

But rather than show their true fear, they put on a brave face, hiding their real emotions from their 'executioners' and giving them no satisfaction of seeing them fearful, which is, I feel, what they would have enjoyed in this particular situation.

The soul came back to the scene of the crime to connect with the souls left here after my earlier SR to forgive them and retract the curse aimed at them just before passing.

This being done, they could all move on in peace hand-in-hand; beautiful!

Having chatted to the souls still here, I invited them to step into the portal which, incidentally, had opened up via the sun breaching the clouds, just as I ended my speech.

Perfect!

Smithills Hall and 'The Penny Has Finally Dropped' ~ 23rd November to 6th December 2019

THE LAST TWENTY-FOUR hours have been most amazing, regarding my ever-increasing capacity to connect with souls visually, but also on all other levels too!

Over the last three weeks I have been troubled with varying degrees of dizziness, culminating in the most challenging episode on the Tuesday evening, the 19th November. This caused some deep concern; in plain terms, it scared me!

Only a while after did I realise this was two-fold:

The dizziness was part of the ascension process helping us raise our vibration to a new level to embrace a 'new world'. This scary bout of dizziness also brought up the fear from a few years ago when I experienced something similar, and at the time I thought I was going to die.

This fear was the issue I needed to accept and let go of, duly done hours later.

This experience was the catalyst which blessed me with deep insight as to my challenge regarding my 'soul purpose' work taking off, having taken four days to come to light.

On Wednesday evening I was just about to turn my laptop off and go to bed, when Yvonne, my dear friend, sent me some healing; I had requested help via healing on Yvonne's divinely created healing page on Facebook a few days earlier. I knew this was a sign for me to get into bed and allow this healing to flow through me.

It was very powerful and I have had no further dizzy spells since. Thursday was a day of rest!

Friday, I felt a big shift had taken place, I felt such a deep peaceful feeling flowing through me; amazing!

Also on Friday, Yvonne had seen my interview with a lady in the USA on 11th November and was kind enough to share her thoughts about it, all so uplifting, boosting my confidence no end.

She also gave me confirmation regarding a SR I had done a few weeks ago, which I spoke about during the interview, which further increased my confidence.

Saturday arrived with even more blessings!

I enjoyed a wonderful walk in nature with Lynn, a dear friend, then came home to ready myself to visit with Janet and Mark before going to meet Jane at Smithills Hall to meet her friend who runs the paranormal investigation which was occurring the same evening.

My catch-up with Janet and Mark was wonderful, all boosting my new-found confidence.

I met Jane at 8pm, we started with a walk around the building's perimeter. During this short excursion I connected with so many souls who had in various ways become trapped outside the hall. Having completed the circle and now back in the car park, I felt such a strong presence near my car. Within moments, Jane heard a noise coming in the direction of the main doorway. As I neared the doorway and to the right, I felt another strong presence.

I then receive information via my angelic friends that the two presences were connected and had partaken in some kind of duel, rendering both their physical 'vessels' dead!

Seconds later I was guided towards a window, where I sensed a young girl had fallen from the upstairs window. Standing below the window I again felt such a strong presence of the little girl receiving additional information about her.

The little girl had blonde curly hair and wore a white/cream dress, lace in a patterned design, and also the age I received for her was three. To receive this much information was a new experience for me but it showed at an early stage what the three weeks of dizziness had instigated; all the above happening within five minutes at most!

A thorough clearing out of my mind was the blessing; all the unnecessary thoughts, chatter, etc. now a distant memory.

All this created room for the information to now flow so easily to me; however, it was now for me to trust all that I had received.

Completely and irrevocably!

Now those two words are the key. I had obviously had some belief in what I was doing and receiving information during each SR, but until now I realise I was seeking confirmation after each one.

A clear sign that I wasn't trusting completely what I had been gifted!

This has been a little stumbling block, if you like.

I have to trust completely what I receive regardless of what the person or persons I relay these messages to, think!

I have known this but haven't, until now, followed through with this knowledge completely!

This wisdom came today, the 24th November, during a visit to Tracey's, a friend and author, who, through conversation, led me to realise this issue was the sole cause of my block or lack to receiving financial abundance!

'Wow!' That is all I can say, 'Wow!'

The penny has well and truly dropped today!
Again, all within the realm of Divine Timing.

Further adding to my increasing confidence, which I need to emit when spreading the word regarding SR.

During our chat Tracey also gave me confirmation regarding a SR I have written about previously, which was lovely to receive, but I now realise I have no need to seek others' confirmation, be it from my angelic friends or earthly friends, from this moment forward I *must* believe:

What I see
Whatever information I receive and
What I feel resonates with me as truth
And to trust this is so!

I returned to Smithills on the 6th December 2019 in the hope of finishing what I had been guided to do. I again walked around the property but in the other direction. I then walked over a little bridge, heading to the Coaching House.

The Coaching House is now a housing complex but the structure of the building has been utilised during the renovations. However, I was unable to walk around this area as I wished to, so my attempts were somewhat thwarted but never mind.

I wasn't meant to do a SR in this area, as I had thought!

Crossing the bridge, I felt the urge to stand still, which I did, soon to be joined by a soul, whose physical body had jumped or had been pushed into the stream below, leaving the soul trapped on the bridge.

These SRs seemed to be very easy to complete on both my visits. I feel the souls here were ready to move on regardless of their experiences at the time of death. I have received no information regarding their demise but I'm fine with that, the main aim is to play my part in helping the souls to move on.

(It is nice to get some background information on the SRs I do but it isn't a necessity.)

I then made my way inside the hall, visiting each room, giving any souls there the time to connect with me.

I did connect with two souls in the main hall and felt my throat tighten as I entered the chapel but having had all those experiences outside on my first visit, I was in some ways expecting the inside to produce more of the same; another example of how expectation can bring feelings of disappointment!

I wasn't disappointed, rather I was surprised at the lack of connection but as I'm aware now, I have connected to those souls who I have agreed to come back to help and also any remnants of my own soul!

Job done; there will be other souls in this building but none I was meant to help, this will be the journey of other souls in other bodies, coming to do their bit, as it were.

The throat issue was part of my soul's past life. Again, I received no information, however I feel my soul was passing through here during a lifetime in the past, whereby a situation occurred, which led to an essence of my soul becoming 'stuck'.

This is as important a piece of my soul to retrieve as any, but if I logged every little essence I've connected to I'd have to write many, many books, leaving very little time to actually do the SRs, hehe!

The essence is when our soul experiences a situation where, over a period of time, our energy builds up. So, the longer we stay in a particular place, let's say our home, our energies will be imprinted there and the stronger our essence will be! We will undoubtedly have become attached to it in some way, whether positive or negative, depending on our experiences while in this place.

This attachment is how an essence is formed. It's simply a build-up of our unique energies, our memory, and depending on the issue or situation, it can be necessary for us to revisit these areas to connect with the essences, to disperse them – a bit like doing a SR but on a lesser scale, but as I say all fragments of our soul are as important to collect to complete the jigsaw of our soul!

The essence issue is further explained in the next piece, which is more of a reconnection to my soul's essence from the past rather than a SR.

Blissfully 'Home Alone' ~ 13th December 2019

I WAS GUIDED to do a meditation, in which I visited a past-life dwelling; this was situated in a mountainous region close to Nepal.

My life as a monk was spent in isolation, living in a cave, seeking the wisdom of the universe and other such things. My soul and its physical form spent many years there, eventually passing due to the cold, freezing to death!

Now I know this sounds gruesome, but by the time this transition occurred we, the body and soul, had attained a level of 'Spiritual Mastery' in as much as being able to block out the cold; this having been mastered during many years of meditation and self-discipline. But alas, the physical body wasn't made to cope with those temperatures, regardless of being able to block out the feelings of coldness.

I returned to the cave to reunite with an essence which had formed while living there. My experiences within and around this cave had helped me raise my vibration, so much so, that just before passing I had attained the level of true peace.

This is how my physical body passed!

Having attained this level, and during my final meditation, I had gone so deep that my physical body simply shut down as my soul ascended.

A wonderful finale to a truly wonderful lifetime!

As I came to from the meditation this morning, I felt such peace and contentment. I had led a simple life living off the land, spending all my time alone and on spiritual learning; it was bliss! I was also blessed with a vision of the scenery around the cave, which was absolutely stunning.

These are the gifts I have reconnected to, the deep sense of peace and contentment but also the divine knowledge I had been blessed with during my isolation in that lifetime.

This divine knowledge, combined with these feelings had been nurtured for years, as if I instinctively knew, one day, I would return for them to help me in the future, which I now thankfully have.

As I write this paragraph, I am overwhelmed with sensations as I simply said, 'Wow', realising this was true; how God works in mysterious, yet truly remarkable ways. Amazing!

We will at some stage be guided to connect with the positive essences which were stored in any specific past life to help us here 'in the now' and that you, as I have, will be physically guided to a certain place, at a certain time, where you may feel familiar yet you have never been there before, to reconnect to your soul's gifts; this will be more so when it's a positive essence.

Just like in a video game, a player will begin, then start to collect certain items along the way so that he/

she may complete the game, or in this case to help us finish this 'Earth experience', part of our souls' journey.

The negative essences are slightly different because these are in need of clearing, sometimes as part of a fully complete SR. I suppose these could be likened to challenges along the pathway to ascension, trying to put a spanner in the works, so to speak.

These negative essences will need some sort of cleansing/healing work done to discard them, akin to an MOT for a car, so we require a tune-up and cleansing every now and then!

For example:
The essences of those who were part of the Black Magic Circle at Rivington I wrote about previously. The more rituals they held there, the stronger their essences built up so the more effort it took to clear the area of those negative essences.

Everything in balance:
The positive essences we reconnect with are gifts to help us through the next period of our journey.

The negative essences we reconnect with are excess baggage we are asked to heal and release; both ultimately positive actions when connecting with each.

There is, however, nothing for you to worry about, only when you are ready to open up to this awareness, will you begin to understand what is happening.

That time will be made clear to you when you begin to seek alternative methods of healing to help you with your well-being.

This is the starting point of your 'awakening'.

158 The 'Final' SR ~ Sometime in 1967 to 1st January 2020

'Wow' is all I can say!

Anyway, last evening, New Year's Eve, I returned home having had an enjoyable day with Debbie.

While making a cuppa a surge of anger came over me and I threw the bin lid across the kitchen, such was the ferocity and swiftness of this anger!

I hadn't realised what I'd done until seeing the bin lid on the floor – 'flabbergasted' is the word to best describe my state at that moment.

I picked up the bin lid, put it back on the bin and continued to make my cuppa feeling slightly embarrassed as I did so; very much out of character for me these days! All this happened within seconds.

Moving on to this morning, New Year's Day: dream experience.

While asleep, I was transported back to '158' (this is the number of the house where I lived for 50+ years) the scene of many an unpleasant experience! I was in mum's bedroom looking up at her from my cot as she and Dad seemed to argue; I didn't see Dad but knew he was there.

Mum repeatedly said something like, 'You're not going to die.' I sensed Mum and Dad were in a state of panic, standing there helpless, waiting for an ambulance/doctor to arrive, while I was involved in a life or death struggle for breath, having what I now believe to be a panic attack. Dream ends!

I woke up and started to understand more of the emotions expressed during the dream.

To witness your second child struggling for life, having already lost your first-born after twenty-four hours; it doesn't bare thinking about!

My experience with the bin last evening replicated the way Dad's anger surfaced just before hitting me with his belt as a nine year old; again, giving me a much better understanding of his actions, making it easier to forgive him!

This dream experience took me back to the most horrific attack, the closest I came to feeling I was going to die, to show me the effects it had on Mum and Dad.

This was also the reason why I have experienced these attacks in recent years. Each episode was an opportunity to see what was waiting to be healed from the past. Only now do I fully understand but I am grateful my angelic friends took care of me while experiencing them.

During this time period, this also occurred...

Around the age of two, for some strange reason I spat at Dad; Dad responded by hitting me. Mum told me about this when she was alive but I only found out why dad hit me during a healing around seven years ago with Yvonne.

Now...

Whether it be in an adult's or a child's body, our soul is ageless, experiencing exactly what it needs to ascend this Earth experience.

My soul was mirror imaging back to Dad his emotional state at the time. Dad was highly frustrated, confused and angry at himself for a number of things; the loss of my brother Jack being the main one.

I was also experiencing the same sort of emotions, for these were some of the emotions which had been imprinted on me since being in the womb. I, as a very young child, was showing anger, frustration, etc., too.

These are the ingredients which created this 'opportunity'.

Whatever the rights and wrongs of this scenario are, our souls had agreed to play out this scene. My actions gave Dad an opportunity to learn from them, but alas, he wasn't spiritually aware enough to see the blessing within my actions.

Are the two experiences connected? I'm not sure, perhaps but it's all conjecture at the moment, but what is most important either way is that I forgive Dad unreservedly!

So...

Having been gifted all of these blessed pieces of the jigsaw, and having been blessed with a level of awareness, I am able now to view each person's 'role' through their emotions/feelings regarding this experience without judgement.

Only now can I bring this family experience to a fruitful conclusion via a SR, but only because I have ascended to a level where I fully accept all that happened was meant to, no one is to blame and to forgive completely is a must.

I have harboured this anger towards Dad for long enough, time to let go and balance the karma so we can all move on to pastures new. This was more of an essence clearing than a soul retrieval.

Again the EC will be a very swift one but the history of one single experience has taken fifty-two years to come to fruition.

I see this as divine timing rather than, why has it taken so long? It has obviously been one of the most unpleasant experiences Dad and I have shared in this life. Hence the reason it has taken a long time for forgiveness to manifest completely on my part.

I can now fulfil my role as SR and finally sever all cords of unhealthy attachment to Mum and Dad; a win-win situation indeed!

Our angelic friends really do work in mysterious yet the most kind and magical ways possible, thank you!

My First 'Self-employed' SR ~ 3rd January 2020

As THE HEADLINE says, this is my first SR for which I was paid, and boy it felt good to be in receipt of remuneration for doing something I truly love!

Yet my priority is to make sure the soul's transition is as comfortable and stress-free as possible, the financial reward is simply that; a reward which will allow me to go further afield regarding SRs to fulfil my soul purpose, while still helping others on their journey.

I visited a lovely family, who live locally. Initially, I chatted with Jackie, Dale and their daughter, inviting them to share their experiences as to the goings-on in their home. It seems, over a period of time, a few situations have occurred, nothing fearful but they have been curious to find out what was going on.

(I was very grateful to Jackie for getting in touch with me!)

The occurrences the family could remember are as follows:

A tight-fitting cupboard door opened on its own.

A glass of Vimto left the window sill and flew across the top of the stairs.

A picture on the wall also travelled from one side of the room to the other.

Dale sensed someone was watching him as he did some work on the skirting boards on the stairs; I'm sure you may have experienced something similar?

Some coins had been moved during the night and while I was there, their son shouted to his mum, something had moved in his room. We went into the bedroom and sure enough, I felt a presence!

Having had a brief chat with Jackie's son Frankie, I assured him I believed what he had told us. We then left the bedroom.

We again chatted at the top of the stairs and just before I went up into the loft, I got a strong message, really it was just one word: grandma.

I mentioned this to Jackie and Dale, and again the word grandma came to mind, further giving me confidence to trust and relay this message to them.

This was definitely Jackie's grandma making herself known; Jackie had known for a while that her father was with her as a guide but hadn't yet connected to her grandmother.

This was one soul mystery solved!

One of the presences I felt during our tour around the house did eventually make itself known to me as Jackie's dad; this I understood during our chat near the end of the SR. Not that this was a soul mystery solved, more a realisation for me this was one of the presences I felt around the house.

I then made my way up into the loft, connecting to a soul who was trapped, having hanged himself; Dale told me about this as we went from room to room.

I spoke to this beautiful soul, inviting him to come with me, so we could help his transition be completed through our SR team, which he inevitably did.

Finally, we returned to the living room and chatted a little more. Katie, Jackie's daughter, asked me about her dad. When she asked this question, I felt a gentle tingling all down my back, signalling that her dad was making his presence felt and was with her.

Another soul mystery solved!

Finally, the soul who had passed in tragic circumstances also made himself known; this beautiful soul was part of Dale's soul.

Again, I received confirmation of this each time I thought about the soul and the extreme occurrences which directly involved Dale via:

The sense of someone watching him.

The picture flying across their bedroom and the Vimto experience, all of which point to the trapped soul making himself known to Dale, more than any other member of the family. So, all the family's questions had been answered – yay!

The other souls were letting their loved ones know they were there for them, that they were not alone and were there to help in any way they could!

Beautiful, because this is where I have been blessed with further SR knowledge.

It was the first SR I had been made aware that some of the souls were family members who had passed and simply wished to make their loved ones aware they were with them.

I had one SR to oversee with my angelic friends, which was completed the same evening.

Joy and happiness aplenty flowed through me, because it really makes my heart sing when I'm able to help in this way, knowing a soul which had been stuck in an illusion for however long, had now taken the courageous steps to move on. To trust what I had done and said and then to trust my SR friends was very humbling and a very satisfying feeling indeed!

On my way home, I was blessed with confirmation that I had done everything I was meant to via a car registration plate, with the numbers 777 on it.

Now, 777 signifies to me that I am well and truly on the right track, but in this instance it was a very clear sign that all had been achieved!

'Between a Rock and a Hard Place' EC and SR ~ 15th January 2020

On this day I was blessed with the opportunity to do another EC, again with a little difference. The home I visited was experiencing slight murmurings from what I thought was a trapped soul over the last few days.

Belle (an alias) the lady who contacted me, acted swiftly, sensing these murmurings would only become more frequent and perhaps disturbing to her children. During our initial chat Belle told me about the couple who lived in this house before she moved in.

The couple, during their time there, had the hardest decision ever to contemplate and eventually make, which created before and after a period of deep sadness, despair, fear, anger a lack of self-worth, etc.!

The lady was expecting a baby but complications had arisen during the pregnancy, leading to the couple being told of the chances of survival.

The essences were those of the gentleman and his wife who had made the decision to have the pregnancy terminated for all their sakes. If their choice was difficult, then the emotions which followed would have been even harder to live with.

Only God knows what emotions were running through the minds of that couple! Whichever decision they made, very challenging experiences would and did ensue.

The doubt, the guilt, the blame and so on, these feelings can and do create a tidal wave of negative experience after negative experience, as I can vouch for from my experiences with Mum and Dad.

During any time of heightened emotive experiences, these energies will be released from their bodies out into the house; the house then soaks up these negative energies, causing the house to remain in a state of negativity.

Unless attended to, these energies, in conjunction with other negative issues which can occur in the future, will only increase the house's negative state, adding to their already fragile, negative state.

My family's home experienced this spiral downwards for over fifty years, all stemming from one situation; that of my brother's passing. Each situation heaped more negativity on the house, the house then holding this energy like a sponge, while we continued to live there.

All the while this growing negativity within the walls, etc. was adding to our combined negative state and took over four months for me to clear it before the house eventually sold.

So, during this particular EC I did a house cleansing as well, using my spiritual tools to cleanse the house of all negative energies, not just the essences.

Belle gave me a tour of the house giving the souls a chance to connect with me. I felt the man's essence strongest downstairs, as Belle told me about a toy which turned itself on three times over a short period.

I do feel as time passed these experiences would have increased. It's due to the fact that Belle, and more so her mother, are more intuitive and understand this sort of spiritual phenomena, so acted a lot sooner!

Upstairs I felt a strong presence in Belle's daughter's room, where she had experienced these goings-on, and again the gentleman and I sensed a more subtle presence of his wife!

I felt distraught while stood in the little girl's bedroom, this added to the pacing Belle's little girl also heard! Which also reminds me, Belle said her little girl heard someone 'talking naughty'. Again, I feel this was the man beating himself up for his part in their decision.

This was the man's main issue, sensing it was more his decision, nudging his partner/wife to end the pregnancy in this unpleasant way, due to fear of how their life would be had they chosen to go through with the pregnancy to the birth.

I added this at a later date (15th June 2020): I do feel a part of the gentleman's soul did actually stay there, simply because he didn't want to let go; hence the noises etc.

When such a catastrophic situation as this occurs, it is quite easy to see why a part of the man's soul wouldn't want to leave the house, feeling he was leaving his child behind.

It has similarities to my mum and dad losing my brother Jack after only twenty-four hours of life.

Having done the EC and connected to the soul who was ready to move on, this wonderful SR and EC for Belle and her family ended.

I still had the final part to complete; this was done later that same evening!

I did ask for confirmation because I really wanted to know that I had fulfilled my part in this SR and EC, having been recommended to Belle via her mum and a very dear friend of mine.

I received it with such clarity, phew!

Essence Clearing and Soul Retrieval
(The Subtle Differences)

I FELT DRAWN to adding this here at this time, to help you as we go through more SRs from here on in.

As I progress doing SRs, the information I receive is becoming more refined, as I will express here and now regarding the above title.

Essence clearing is the basis for every experience I have had and will have involving SR, it can be done even when there are no souls to be moved on.

Essence clearing is the spiritual 'removal' of built-up energies/memories caused by a situation or experience, mostly negative but can also be from a positive experience too.

The strength of the essence is based purely on the extremeness of the experience and the length of time which has passed, on the build-up to, during and after the experience...

Our soul knows when something is coming into our physical reality, so the physical body will begin to sense/ feel emotions coming up even before the experience or situation has happened.

An essence can be nurtured anywhere inside or outside; it is simply based on the amount of time spent in a specific place and the type of emotion which creates the essence. Positive or negative!

This can be anger, fear, happiness, etc., any sort of emotion you can think of; these are the ingredients which form an essence.

There is an additional twist to the essence issue.

I believe there is an instance where a soul can become trapped by the essence/memory more than the physical experience, due to the ferocity and swiftness of a specific experience which can create very extreme emotions, very quickly.

This happened to me, when having to vacate my home in a very swift and sudden way. Shock was the essence which held that part of my soul in the house.

This situation had to be attended to when Dad passed in February 2016 before I was able to move on, on my journey.

I put the house up for sale, which was bought by a cash buyer but took four months to complete. During this time, I became a little frustrated at the length of time it took to complete but now I understand why it did.

It took this long for me to completely heal and clear the house of the essences which had been nurtured there for over fifty years; the essences of Mum, Dad and myself, our combined memories.

I also reconnected to the part of my soul which stayed in the house and needing to clear the essence of shock from my last few hours living with dad. I wasn't completely aware of my SR work at this time otherwise the time span for the sale of the house would have been much less.

I didn't live in the house when Dad passed, I just kept popping back to clear his stuff and the furniture, etc.

When the sale completed, I was assured my work had also been completed!

SR Done While Sleeping ~ 31st January 2020

A VERY BRIEF explanation because I only received limited information...

On waking I remembered what seemed to be a large hole, perhaps purposely dug or even a bomb may have created it.

There were body parts strewn all around this area.

I received the number '100', believing this to be the amount of souls involved with this tragedy and the number of souls we as a team were able to help move on.

And the final piece of information was the place: Helmand Province.

When looking it up, I found that it is in Afghanistan and an area where lots of conflict had and still is taking place.

It's hard to distance myself from these occurrences but I must if I am to be of most help, perhaps this is why this particular SR was done in this way.

The day after, I did search for anything to do with Helmand Province and any news; the first piece I was guided to 'spoke' of one hundred people being killed in a specific attack, this was enough to confirm to me what had been shown in the dream had happened.

I seem to be doing more of this type of 'astral' travel while sleeping, doing SR work in places which at this time are unsafe for me to visit physically.

Boleskine House, Scotland, SR and EC ~ 8th-19th February

2020

I TRAVELLED TO Stirling in Scotland the day before and then set off for Boleskine House on the Saturday morning.

This is a place where I have felt a great desire to visit to help clear the area and help any souls move on in general and on a personal level. This house was once owned by Aleister Crowley a man who allegedly dabbled in dark 'ceremonial rituals' amongst other things!

This was the next step on my journey and something I couldn't overlook.

It took almost four hours from Stirling, a little longer than I had thought and perhaps a trip I may have had less passion to take on, had I known the time it would take to get there!

Anyway, I finally arrived and found the lay-by which Joe, a member of the Boleskine House Foundation, told me about.

During my trip I had received a message from Yvonne to use rock salt when doing my clearing ritual, to use holy water and sprinkle it around the area, and say the

Lord's Prayer also when doing my work.

This, along with other snippets of guidance from friends, had me a tad concerned.

Had I let myself in for something I couldn't handle?
Well, I would soon find out!

In addition to the advice from Yvonne, I was also guided by Archangel Michael to take my Reiki Masters crystal - a rose quartz crystal which had been blessed by Yvonne and the angels during an angelic reiki attunement.

I took my pyrite globe, another rose quartz crystal, and a beautiful pair of angel wings gifted to me by another dear friend Jody, which she had blessed with reiki energy, and last but by no means least I took a bag of sage!

I had no holy water but improvised and used some bottled water then some rain water asking God to bless both - which 'she' did very graciously - sprinkling this all around the house, the gardens and the stable blocks at the back.

Perhaps I felt a little overprotected but as I was to find out I needed every ounce of help, via these tools, my SR teammates, guides and the reiki symbols I also used.

I will admit I underestimated the power of the energies here at Boleskine; I felt such abhorrent acts had been carried out here, without going into them!

I also felt I was more reliant on my angelic friends too; all in all I felt I was a little disrespectful all round!

A very valuable lesson learnt!

I soon found out to my amazement the force and density of negativity around this area, the fear I felt as I left my car and throughout this SR shocked me, if I'm honest.

This fear will have been building up since the very first ritual took place, plus everything else which had occurred under the black magic banner since, and also from other periods of time, when war, and conflict were rife.

So, the depth of fear I felt was most understandable!

Having left the car and aligned myself after the shock of the fear which greeted me, I looked for the entrance to the house via a gap in the fence; again, via Joe's guidance.

Now, before visiting Boleskine, I had to ask for permission and sign a waiver before being allowed entrance with it being a private property.

While walking up and down the road, the energy was so thick with fear, fear of many who had perished here over many, many years!

I felt other unwelcoming energies too, which had me slightly concerned but I was here to do a job so I forged on, finding the gap in the wire fence, almost causing myself undue harm, as I had to limbo under the wire and then proceeding to enter the land where the house and two stable blocks stood; all having seen better days.

Immediately I lit some sage and began to approach the house, sensing souls just outside the back door and to the left as I looked at it. This corner of the house was where I felt most activity had taken place, within the house as a whole; some sort of underground room.

Much more had gone on in the stable at the back,

which you will read about further into this piece!

It took me many attempts to light the sage, obviously 'someone' didn't want me to succeed, but eventually I did and was able to cleanse this part of the house while saying the Lord's Prayer and having called upon my angelic friends well before starting this SR.

I then moved round the side of the house and onto the front lawn, walking around as much of the perimeter as I was able to. Again, sensing various souls, using sage and calling upon my angelic friends when walking round a tree in a secluded area; thankfully they moved on with ease.

I then walked around the house once more with sage and again saying the Lord's Prayer but still feeling such powerful energies as I did so. I then headed to the first stable block, where surprisingly there was no real cleansing needed.

Maybe this lulled me into a false sense of security because when approaching the stable block at the back, wow the air was thick with negativity; so powerful!

I had to urge myself to do this part of the SR; such was the build-up of fearful energies.

Again, I must admit, it really surprised me how powerful they were. I thank God for this experience because I will do my very best never to underestimate any SR I do from here on in.

My solar plexus was doing cartwheels, my sacral chakra in turmoil, but I had to move through this because these were deep emotions which needed to be released on a personal level. They were all feelings from past experiences, obviously unpleasant ones but this in part was why I was here.

I had to go through this to set my soul free, otherwise I would be unable to move on in this lifetime.

The stable block was where the deadly deeds took place and over a much longer period of time, longer than I had envisaged!

In addition, I was 'told' by my guides and teammates that something had happened in the past where a ritual had been initiated, opening a portal in the process but hadn't been closed, allowing all sorts of negative entities to enter this world.

The closing of this portal was mainly done by my SR teammates while I held the space in a physical way, focusing on doing all I could to cleanse and clear what I was here to do.

As my teammates worked on closing the portal, I saged around the stable block three times; I said the Lord's Prayer a few times; I talked almost incessantly in the hope these souls would trust me regardless of why they were here, whether for good or bad, and I called on my angelic help and the ultra violet angels to constantly work on clearing this heaviness!

At times it took me all of my strength and faith to stay put and finish this SR.

I connected to a very frightened soul round the back of the stable, hiding in the undergrowth, the hours and days leading up to his passing, let's just say they were most unpleasant, hence his soul being rooted to the spot!

I worked on this one building alone for over an hour, most of this time spent on one specific area behind a door I was unable to access, with a sign on it saying NO ENTRY.

This sign couldn't have been more apt; behind this

door was where all the unpleasantness had taken place.

It took me all my strength to face this but I did, I had to!

As I worked on this room, I saw a black figure leave the main door, trying to make a run for it, but as with the other souls, he would have moved on before I left, otherwise my stay would have been extended.

During this SR I used a full bag of sage; unheard of in any of my other SRs.

I was so glad of the spiritual support and guidance from my friends and I am so glad I was able to do what I went there to do, regardless of the challenges!

I did, however, bring a soul back with me, part of my soul's journey which had become stuck, a build-up of his energies, leaving a trail so Shanti and I would find and connect with him one day. It soon became apparent I had more than one soul returning with me!

The souls who came with me, the protagonist and the part of my soul did, as of the 15th February, move on via a SR. As you will read in a little more detail, I needn't have brought these souls home with me, but we live and learn!

Prior to my visit to Boleskine, my soul, Shanti, visited this area with Archangel Michael and other angels from our SR team while I slept, to prepare this area even before I thought of coming here.

I also consciously sent healing light to this area too; all in preparation for this visit. During the whole SR there were fearful feelings coming up within me but as I said I was there to do a job. I wasn't going to let these feelings get the better of me.

Many times during the SR I saged myself, such was

the intensity of the energies, especially around the stable block right at the back almost in the wooded area. This is the EC part of the clean-up, clearing the energetic build-up rather than the souls themselves.

Having returned home I had a chat with Yvonne, telling her of my adventures. She told me that each time I do SR and bring the trapped souls home with me, it is showing me I still have a lack of self-worth.

I was quite surprised at this but do now understand why this information is true.

I feel it's all about me trusting in what I do, and to bring these souls home with me seems to appease a part of me that seeks approval and the need to show those who invite me into their homes to do SR that they are getting their money's worth.

It has also revealed an attachment to loss, especially when the SR involves a part of my soul not wanting to let go of it, when in truth letting go is the best thing to do for all parties.

So, to summarise:
- A lack of self-worth
- A lack of trust
- The fear of loss

These are all issues my brief but very informative chat with Yvonne brought up, which need to be attended to so I can step onto the next rung of my SR ladder.

The outcome is thus:
I have no need to bring any more souls back home with me, I can now enhance the SRs with the increased

knowledge I have and help the souls move on at the point of connection.

This will save me a lot of unnecessarily spent energy by bringing them home and able to do more SRs without getting too fatigued – yay!

If I understood every nuance regarding SR at the very beginning, I would have missed out on so many amazing experiences. It was for me to remember gradually as it will be for you.

It's all a learning curve!

It's imperative I experience everything, so I have an answer or at least some guidance which will help you on your journey, should you need help.

You will then have someone to connect with, be it through this book or any SR courses I will be running, or indeed by talking to me one to one as it were, or someone else altogether to share your amazing SR experiences.

Another personal gift I have been blessed with stemming from my chat with Yvonne is that whatever I have written in the previous pages, is exactly what I knew at the time, using the gifts I knew about at the time, rather than beating myself up for not knowing what I know now, if you see what I mean!

This will also leave me with an abundance of spare energy to use in much more productive ways, again, yay!

Yes, resting and recovery is necessary to do SR work, but this additional information will allow me to do more SRs with the need to do less resting, a 'Brucie bonus' indeed!

I have also said to myself, and anyone who would

listen, before going to Scotland to do this SR it would take me to a new level... It has but boy in so many magical ways I could never have imagined, yay!

Thank you, God my SR teammates and my friends who gave me additional guidance to complete the most magical, challenging, adventurous SR thus far!

19th June 2020:

Since doing this SR I have been shown time and again how much of a challenge it was and the good that we as a SR team have caused through our combined efforts.

I feel *so* blessed to be a part of a wonderful team!

Braemar SR ~ 3rd August 2016 to 21st February 2020

I HAD DONE the odd SR before this experience but I feel the darkness regarding the experience here in Braemar would have been too much for me to handle on my first visit, but I did get a taste of what it would uncover, as you are about to find out!

The Boleskine SR brings completion to an ongoing issue which I first connected to during a flying visit to Braemar in Scotland a few years ago.

As I arrived in Braemar looking for somewhere to stay the night, I stopped at the Braemar Lodge hotel. On entering, it was very dimly lit.

I asked the lady did she have any rooms available, she said she would look and went into another room. While waiting for the lady to return, I felt an overwhelming unpleasantness and a strong desire to leave the hotel as soon as possible. I managed to hang on until the lady returned with the news; she had no available rooms that night.

Talk about relieved!

I then changed my mind about staying in Braemar and headed further afield.

Just as I was exiting Braemar, still with these very unpleasant feelings fresh in my mind, my friend Debbie rang me; it turns out at the perfect time, because our conversation took my mind off what had just occurred!

A few months later I was by-passing Aberdeen heading South, I saw a sign for Braemar, instantly I knew I had to go but didn't want to. I got as far as the next roundabout and turned around heading for Braemar.

In Braemar, I again visited the same hotel but this time it was much brighter. I again asked if there was a room available, this time there were two but I felt I needed to see them both before deciding.

I didn't fancy either of them to be honest, they were lovely rooms but I felt that whatever was happening, I felt no need to stay overnight, for whatever reason!

Since the first visit, Braemar has been loitering in the shadows.

I have never got to the bottom of this beautiful village and its 'dark secrets' but hopefully with this SR it seems to have opened up a channel for me to access information that will bring Braemar to completion too.

Since my fleeting visits to Braemar I've come to understand my soul had a very unpleasant lifetime there and the reason for my second visit was to allow the part of my soul to connect with me. I didn't stay in the hotel long enough for the soul to connect with me the first time around.

It was necessary for me to spend some time in the hotel to allow the soul to gain trust in me to leave with me, at the second time of inviting, to help it move on at a suitable time. I had very little idea of the SR necessary, simply because of the dark energies surrounding it. I did feel energies change around me while in one of the bedrooms but thought nothing of it.

Over the years, I have been gifted more information about my soul's life in Braemar and can understand how this lifetime corresponds with my soul's lifetime in the Boleskine house area.

Different time periods in history but each life caused my soul to experience what I feel to be the worst experiences one could imagine; perhaps this is why I was given no details about Boleskine during my time there and since!

I have done part of a SR at Braemar but only via 'dream-state'. I feel all that needed to be done was done this way, because I wasn't ready to do a SR there in the physical, so to speak!

It did help me understand the following very vivid dream I have had a few times during my life.

I was running through a wooded area, being chased! I was in so much fear. I was trying to shout for help but no words were coming from my mouth. I have never been shown the ending but it wasn't a happy one, that's for sure!

My mum and dad in this lifetime were very wealthy. This proved to be their downfall for they were killed because of this, leaving the child, my soul, to be looked after by unscrupulous people, dare I say!

The people in whose care my soul was entrusted were the same people who murdered my parents, leading to the child being abused until the day he too was murdered.

This is what I was shown during the dream, the

running away led to the child being murdered there and then! The people who did this then received all the wealth for themselves, with no relatives, etc. alive.

So, it was all about fear, betrayal, trust, etc. in this life and so it has been regarding the Boleskine SR. This is where I realise I needed to go, to bring this whole issue to an end, this is why I felt the fear when moving around – Boleskine, and more so around the back of the stables where all the horrors happened in that life!

Having had very limited experience of SR on my first and second visits to Braemar, I had little understanding regarding what was required for me to help this soul, until he made himself known to me today the 21st February 2020! This didn't stop the child's soul from joining me on my second visit and has been with me ever since!

As I write the above paragraph, I feel a very strong presence at my back, I utter a couple of colourful words, shall I say, in my surprise or shock.

Not until this very moment, do I realise the strong presence was the child's soul from Braemar! The souls from Boleskine have long gone but the child's soul has been waiting patiently for the jigsaw to be almost complete before making his presence felt; such was his fear of his prolonged abuse and ending in Braemar.

Only now am I knowledgeable enough to cope with any further information that may come to light regarding Braemar, having now done the SR at Boleskine and what still needs to be done to 'clear' Braemar!

This is another example how you have almost certainly connected to a part of your soul, during this present lifetime without any idea of the soul connection.

This soul will wait patiently until you have sufficiently awakened so you can help them.

Everything happens within the realm of divine timing!

When you reach this level of awareness, whether you choose to call upon my services or someone like me or by gaining the necessary knowledge, you can help these souls move on yourself.

There is nothing to fear if this is so!

I have a SR to finish this evening: 21st February 2020... Wow, amazing!

This will help to bring an end to my self-worth issues, for they were multiplied drastically through these lifetimes which my soul, Shanti, has experienced now the light has been well and truly shone on these limiting emotions; time for these to be completely healed and for the beautiful soul to move on!

Additional information:

On the 29th February 2020, I received some news from a dear friend while visiting her for a chat. A soul who unbeknown to me had attached itself to me at Boleskine House! During our chat the soul had relocated to my friend's house, where she helped the soul to swiftly move on.

Now, in the past I would have felt guilty when being told this but I now know this was all meant to be. I had protected myself as much as I could before, during and after the Boleskine SR, but even so, if a soul is meant to connect with me or you, it will regardless of how much protection I or you 'put up'; it's part of our soul agreement!

The soul was part of my friend's soul journey and had come back for her to assist the soul to move on.

The Boleskine/Braemar SRs have been totally amazing in so many ways for me.

I have learnt and remembered a great deal to take into any SR work I do in the future, enhancing the outcomes in easier yet more complete ways, without taking its full toll on me.

Again, this is a win-win situation for all, for it means I will be able to do more SRs, requiring less recovery time – yay!

Additional Information:

WHAT I AM about to write happened and ended in a very *positive* way, so there is no need to become concerned!

As I write this additional piece on the 29th March 2020, we are in a worldwide partial lockdown, a 'virus' causing this situation (hopefully by the time this book comes out, the truth of this matter will be known to more people, however this is not for me to expand on).

Initially seen by some as devastating to the human race but for others, we – the 'lightworkers' of this world – know it's the beginning of a 'New Age', all part of bringing this world back into balance and awakening those who were still asleep!

I had a chat with a friend, who is more updated with this info than me. I prefer to keep out of it and stay calm but the chat shone light on the fact that there have been 'dark beings' and 'light beings' in a tussle to bring this world into a new phase of reality.

The 'virus' in my belief has been created by those dark forces but has backfired somewhat, for their actions come from a base of fear. Its creation will eventually bring the world together more as a family, with help from very powerful light beings; a bit like *Star Wars*, if you like!

Why am I telling you this?

Well, the work I did at Boleskine was more important than I first thought. I knew I was going to face some fears with the area known for black magic occurring there but never thought it was as powerful as it has turned out to have been. The portal I mentioned earlier was left open on purpose, as a portal for dark forces to enter.

So, my mission was a very important one and one which gave me a huge confidence boost at the perfect time. I am just so honoured and filled with joy that I was able to do my bit to help instigate this worldwide change.

Realising how powerful an area Boleskine was, but is no more, after my SR teammates and I did our thing; cleansing, clearing and closing down the portal so no more dark beings can enter.

The dark forces of which I write are simply souls who have yet to awaken, and through their own fears have created unpleasant circumstances in various ways to keep hold of their power, control and financial hold over the masses; it is just a part of their soul's journey.

It is also possible these people believe what they are doing is normal. During their childhood they may have been 'abused' in some way, physically, mentally or emotionally, abandoned, ridiculed, or simply felt unloved, or any other actions which could cause them to seek retribution on their families or anyone in the vicinity.

They are coming from a place of pain and its for us to forgive their actions; a tall order in some respects but this is the only way we can move forward as a 'human race'.

Their fear will eventually be their downfall. They may see it in this way but I view it as a way to help them awaken. During their journey, through their actions and spoken words they have created much karma for themselves to work through as well! I know this at first hand with what my soul has experienced on its journey!

They have a choice: to learn from this period of time or keep going through the same lesson but sooner or later they will see the 'truth' of who they are and in what relation they are to us.

Because, my friend, we are all connected, we are all brothers and sisters, we are all part of the 'oneness' throughout the universe and beyond!

For yours truly, it is to continue to do these SRs without ego but knowing I and my soul are playing an important role to help those souls trapped for however long.

This is my job and I will do it to the best of my ability!

Bee 'Crossing Over' SR ~ 22nd February 2020

THIS OCCURRED VIA a series of events leading me to connect with this beautiful soul.

On the Friday, I was asked by a friend would I be able to drop her off in Bolton; obviously I said yes!

Now on the day of the SR and having dropped my friend off, I received a thought: *Shall we go and have a walk around Queens Park in Bolton?*

So off I drove, arriving and setting off on a walk which would amaze me completely. At various points of my walk, my beautiful friends in the form of magpies illuminated the path they wished me to follow.

This happened three or four times until I came across a bee on the path itself. I bent over to look at this angel, firstly a little surprised to see a bee this early in the year and in this cold weather but here he was!

He hardly moved and at that moment I felt useless, unable to save my friend, but as with the other SR involving a bee I was here to see them safely transition and help their souls move on. I know this to be true because I had no water with me, no sugar, nothing that would help revive this bee.

This SR was slightly different in the fact that the bee was still alive, albeit barely.

After the momentary feeling of uselessness, I realised I was here to help the bee transition, move on in peace, a bit like someone sitting by a loved one's bed who is ready to pass.

I was here to help this angel do just this
and so blessed to be so!

So, having gathered myself and my thoughts I proceeded to talk to the bee, saying a prayer, inviting angels to be here to assist with his transition and to help ease his state while going through this transition, all to make his transition a smooth and peaceful one.

I feel this is where a great many souls can and do become trapped during the transition period, fear can surface at any time, as we all know, and we can also imagine when taking our last breaths this can be a very stressful and fearful time.

Having no idea what's going to happen when our last breath is taken can be very frightening indeed! However when we awaken we will come to realise our soul is everlasting and that we simply move on to another realm/world.

I thank my angelic friends for this insight, receiving it as I began to write this paragraph, thank you!

Back to our beautiful friend...

I was there in total for around five minutes and only left when I saw a gentleman with a dog walking along the path towards me. I sensed my angelic friends were telling me I had done all I was here to do and that it was time to go.

Again, I'm in such awe of my angelic friends, how they guided me to arrive at a specific place, at a very specific time to do what I did, it never ceases to blow me away!

Garstang Mind, Body, Spirit SR ~ 8th March 2020

THIS ROAD TRIP had been arranged for a few days but without any expectation of what would happen and who would I meet.

On arrival, the venue was in a lovely setting and the energies were mostly positive!

As always when visiting events like this, I seem to be guided to connect with specific people. This time was no exception. I met up and chatted with one relatively new friend and made a deep connection with another.

The lady in question, I will name Julia (an alias), I connected with as I stood in the queue waiting to enter the show. First, I went to see my dear friend Jody to see how she was getting on and to drop off a copy of my book; she had a stall selling crystals, etc., a very gifted lady!

I then had a walk round and came upon Julia. We had a brief chat before someone was in need of assistance on her stall, so I made myself scarce and said I would see her later.

An hour later, I was guided to Julia's stall and again a chat ensued. A longer chat this time, with hugs being shared, she did seem very familiar; this would be confirmed later when at home.

The chat all told lasted around half an hour and our initial chat around ten minutes. I tell you this because this was the length of time I needed to be in close proximity to Julia for a specific situation to take place!

This was to allow a part of Julia's soul to connect with me (the taxi part again). We had obviously had at least one past life together, ending in an unpleasant way.

During our two chats, Julia's soul felt comfortable enough to join with me, however I had no idea her soul had connected with me! Yes, during our chats I felt energies around me, especially when talking about my SR book, but again took no real notice.

When the 'exchange' had been completed and the chat ended, it was time for me to bid farewell to the show and my friends there.

Back home, having had a really lovely day. I was then blessed with two beautiful rainbows – the cherry on top of the cake for me during a day of such joy.

I settled down to watch a film and then went to bed having had a fantastic day. I hadn't bargained for what was to happen next though!

The film I watched was called *Dark Shadows*, a sort of comedy horror film, but the ending was the signal for a SR to take place a little later.

Briefly the film was about a witch who had cursed a man, turning him into a vampire where he became immortal. The witch loved the man but he couldn't reciprocate, hence the witch placing a curse upon him! Rejection was the issue; being unable to accept his decision.

The witch cast a spell on the man's true love; she goes over the edge of a cliff to her death.

Hell hath no fury like a woman scorned!

In the film this scenario plays out again two centuries later, but the ending brings about an end to the curse.

The witch is killed and while the man's true love is again heading towards the edge of the cliff about to go over the edge, he gets there in time to fall with her, and on landing he sinks his teeth into her neck turning her into a vampire too!

This is the part of the film I felt energies in my room, especially when at the end the vampire said, 'My curse has finally been broken.'

As I wrote the above line the light in my room flickered vigorously and I went tingly all over; I took this as confirmation!

This film was another way my angelic friends chose to show me what had happened between Julia's soul and part of my soul Shanti in that lifetime.

These two trapped souls were now ready to move on and this film showed me what the issue was.

It was the best way for me to understand the issue of the past life, however it played out.

It didn't take too long for me to put two and two together and realise the energies I felt in my room were those of Julia's soul and until that very moment I had no idea the soul exchange had taken place!

A SR was required!

I refrained from asking too many questions this time, allowing the information to come to me as and when it was meant to.

I then instigated the SR by calling my teammates in to help but also the Lords of Karma made themselves known, and Lady Guinevere!

A curve ball indeed; it was for me to trust their being present was a necessary part of this SR.

The Lords of Karma are a group of powerful ascended masters. They appear during a healing or SR to play their part in releasing those souls involved, who have attained karmic balance.

Lady Guinevere is associated with Merlin, King Arthur, etc., but is an ascended master in her own right connected to true love amongst other things.

The SR gave me my first opportunity to use my new-found knowledge to bring a swift and conclusive outcome to this situation.

I spoke momentarily to Julia's soul, sensing there was a feeling of apprehension regarding her actions.

Forgiveness was also necessary from both souls for this SR to be successful too. I sensed this happened easily because I now know, whatever happened for this curse to have been created our souls have experienced both sides of the coin:

The cursed and the curser!

Again, without sounding like a broken record, it's all part and parcel of our souls' journey, yours and mine!

Anyway, I then called upon my angelic friends to create a Circle of Light around me, wide enough to surround any other souls who were there too. At intervals during the SR I asked my angelic friends to increase the intensity of the light until all souls moved on. Within minutes the SR had successfully been completed.

Job done, so time for bed without needing to stretch the SR out, amazing!

'Up There' SR ~ 11th March 2020

WHILST THIS IS *not* a SR, it is a piece that will give hope to you if you encounter any doubt along your own unique SR path.

This is the title of a film and in it held some divine blessings of reassurance and confirmation for me and for you if you need any.

For me I was blessed with actual physical evidence how soul retrieval takes place without having the visual clarity necessary.

> I see very little but with each SR I am getting
> more through visually!

The film revolved around three actors who had all passed over.

One was a carer whose job was to wait for those souls to pass over then help them to move on in a similar fashion as I do.

The other two souls were involved in an incident, which left one killed in a car crash and the other through his injuries, also passed!

The carer was waiting at the hospital entrance to connect with the soul who had caused the crash, to help him move on. The carer was assisted by the third soul involved in this film but the third soul had no idea who they were waiting for and what this soul had caused.

When the soul arrived, he ran as soon as he saw the carer and other soul, because he recognised the soul was involved in the crash. He ran due to fear, shame, guilt, etc., perhaps a combination of these emotions.

As the film progressed, I started to see the gift for me unfold, to the point where, the two souls came together, each knowing what had occurred, the carer having done his job made himself scarce.

The soul killed in the crash forgave the soul causing the crash and by doing so set himself free, which helped the other soul to forgive himself; beautiful!

They were both able to move on in peace, all assisted by the carer. I suppose the carer's role was similar to my role in our SR team.

To see this unfold visually was a true gift indeed!

This has been the miraculous ending to a few SRs I have done, the one at Flodden comes to mind...

As with the two souls in this film, so too at Flodden and other places I have done SR work, forgiveness was offered and accepted.

At Flodden, I sensed and had a knowing that at least some of those who fought in the battle moved on with their counterparts, hand-in-hand, so to speak.

To visually see that happen would have been such an amazing sight but I do feel it's only a matter of time when I do a SR and I see this occur.

I can't wait!

I simply haven't had the visual clarity to see it happen yet. I have felt it and trusted the knowing feeling within me as I brought those SRs to a most amicable end, but through this film I have been shown what happens and know I should continue to trust myself and my guides.

It has given me a very timely boost regarding what I have done and what I am about to do during many, many more SRs from here on in – yay!

A Magical 'Self' SR ~
12th March 2020

THIS MORNING, AROUND 7am, I did what turned out to be a very powerful self-healing, experiencing a big release from the left side of my stomach, right at the end of the healing!

This was just the beginning of an amazing series of events leading up to the SR. By 10am, I was in the cinema awaiting the film *Dark Waters* to begin; I wasn't sure I was meant to be there but by the time the film finished I knew I had been in the right place.

It's a film about a lawyer who uncovers a large company's indiscretions, shall I say, a film based on true events. Now, this film brought up emotions within me, shame, guilt, fear, etc., which brought a little tearful emotion out. It was showing me that my soul has experienced a lifetime where 'money was king' and everything else was secondary, this is why the emotions came out as they did.

Now, I may have said before, our soul will experience both sides of the coin during its journey of discovery, but I feel the emotion which surfaced today was because my soul had most recently played the role of 'baddie', the one to cause, through his obsession with money, others to be effected in unpleasant ways.

So, it has been fresh in my mind, memories of this lifetime still residing within me at a cellular level and also part of my soul having connected with me from this lifetime, which I had no idea about, until this afternoon!

All of which needed immediate attention, to accept, release and let go of all memories, to help this part of my soul move on.

However, I had no idea about this until I ventured into nature after the film, sitting in a very secluded spot, taking my shoes and socks off, placing my feet firmly on the ground and meditating.

Only while meditating did I get the thought to ask my SR team to join me and place a ring of their divine light around the area in which I sat. During this meditation I saw two butterflies, again quite surprising for the type of weather we were having but obviously they were divine signs for me.

The soul retrieval again was very swift once I understood why each part of today had occurred and the gifts received from each.

I was able to conclude, with help from my angelic friends in nature, etc., that a SR would bring to an end these negative memories from my cellular being and also allow a part of my soul to move on, opening the gateway for Jeffrey/Shanti to move forward in this present life.

Why?

Well, the core issue regards money and how it can corrupt even the best-intentioned person or persons! To realise my soul has focused on money and having done some unpleasant things to manifest money, regardless of how it would affect friends and loved ones, brought up the shame, guilt, fear, etc.

Fear that something or someone may come from the past to scupper our present life. Now, I know this will never happen but these emotions which were within me would have kept dragging me back into the fear, without any idea why.

This would never have allowed me to move forward in the here and now so they had to go.

By releasing, healing, accepting, trusting and finally letting go of these emotions, memories, etc. can Jeffrey/Shanti freely move forward to fulfil our destiny through SR work, accepting the financial rewards which come with it, without any fear attached. Which we deserve!

And to do this, in a most idyllic spot in nature, with the sun peeking through the clouds at the most perfect moments, the wind brisk enough to help blow away these cobwebs, the constant sound of a stream running beside me, and a myriad of nature angels all helping me to bring this issue to an end was simply an experience I will never forget!

Why did I add this to a SR book?

Well, if you ever take up this sort of work you will at some point attain a level where you connect with all the relevant information which will help you understand the complexities of a full SR, rather than just doing a SR ad lib, so to speak. Helping to heal your soul's past in the process.

When you experience a complete SR like this one, you will hopefully feel as I have, so blessed to see it come together in the way our angels and guides support us every step of the way to bring these SRs to an amicable ending!

'Two-in-One' SR ~
1st April 2020

I HAD JUST finished a wonderful walk in nature and now back at my car, phone turned on, I receive messages replying to posts I had put on Facebook.

One message stood out a mile, a reply from Nancy, a lady living in Cork, Ireland.

Sometimes we can connect with people and it seems like we've known them for aeons; this was one of those magical connections!

We chatted about lots of things throughout the day, until hitting upon what I do regarding work, as in my SR work.

Nancy told me a few things about herself and that she has experienced various souls in her house but wasn't sure how to fully help them move on.

Nancy also told me she was a very active person until four years ago when she fell, rendering her almost housebound, a massive change of life for anyone experiencing something of that magnitude. The fall affected her lower back, pelvis, hips and knees; more recently it's just her left hip and knees.

Nancy felt her fall and the issues around it were in

some way connected to her ancestors' past experiences, likened to a 'hereditary' issue. I will add that it's also connected to parts of her soul which had become trapped.

(I have added a detailed explanation at the end of these two SRs to help you understand what hereditary is and an example via the issue of money.)

Anyway, back to Nancy…

As our conversation continued, I began to ask her the following questions:

Me: *Are the souls making any noises?*

Nancy: *If they are, they're doing it in a subtle way!*

Me: *Have you a sense of how many there are?*

Nancy: *About seven or eight is just coming to mind but that's the first number I felt.*

A good example of how to trust your intuition, as in truth there can be any amount of souls with us at any time, so don't discount your feelings.

Back to our conversation…

Nancy: *I just started using a pendulum and asked was there a soul here with the same injury and got a 'yes'. I also asked the soul was it willing to heal and move on; again I got a 'yes'.*

Me: *It needs to offer forgiveness.*

Nancy: *Oh, they need my forgiveness as well, oh goodness Jeffrey, thank you so much!*

As Nancy mentioned the forgiveness, I told her forgiveness is sometimes necessary from both sides for a SR to be a complete success.

If, through your chat with a soul(s) when doing your own SR you can both forgive each other's actions,

212

> then you are ready to let go of the issue and the
> soul(s) trapped can move on to find peace!

I also explained about Archangel Michael, guiding Nancy to call upon him for help to create a portal for this and any other soul within her home that is ready to move on.

As we surfed through this SR I started to realise this was a true blessing for me, being shown yet another way for me and my angelic teammates to help trapped souls move on.

I am *so* honoured and grateful to be doing this work on God's/Goddess's behalf with such amazing teammates...

Thank you! Thank you! Thank you!

'Two in One" SR Pt 2 ~ 6th April 2020

I HAVE HAD another informative conversation via Facebook with Nancy, bringing two past lives our souls had shared together, both involving tragic endings.

Yesterday morning I had what I term as a dream experience, knowing my soul had been on a journey. I woke with this information in my mind:

Ireland ~ Romany ~ suicide ~ family feud
New York ~ a gentleman, well known for his manners
~ consumption (tuberculosis)

Quite cryptic signs at first glance but as I chatted with Nancy today, boy how the magic between us has shone light upon these lifetimes with such synchronicity; we certainly have got a powerful bond/connection!

We have been able to unravel these lifetimes bringing up the issues which needed to be attended to, so those parts of our souls trapped in New York and Ireland can be set free to move on.

I first ask Nancy some questions:

Me: *Have you been to New York?*

Nancy: *Yes, many times, almost living there at one point!*

I asked her this because during one of her visits she will have connected to the part of her soul, and perhaps mine too, which was trapped in the past life.

Me: *Can you ask your pendulum if one or both of the souls committed suicide and were they Romanies?*

Nancy: *Both were Romanies!*

As Nancy said this I went all tingly, giving me confirmation of what she said was correct!

During these first moments of our chat, I sensed my soul was connected to at least one of the lives I was questioning her about.

Me: *I'm a little confused, Nancy, can you ask if the two souls were both Romanies again please, just to confirm?*

Nancy: *They were both Romanies and in the same lifetime.*

Me: *Can you ask if the lifetime took place in Ireland?*

Nancy: *Yes, and both committed suicide (at the same time) and in the very same place where I live now; wowza huh* (Nancy's words).

This life, it transpires our souls were Romanies but from different families, who just happened to be feuding. Our souls' love for each other knew no bounds but the pressure from both families took its toll! Both souls felt the only way out was to commit suicide by way of jumping off a cliff!

The ending of this lifetime was in some ways as tragic as the infamous *Romeo and Juliet*, a true romance destined to fail.

To continue...

Nancy: *I'm asking if the souls are happy now.*

Me: *I was tingling all over as I read your message, Nancy!*

Nancy: *Awesome, I feel good about it too!*

Moments later my heart began to warm considerably, I took this to be further confirmation that Nancy and I, through our chat, had brought this lifetime, this SR, to the brink of closure.

Again, there is little to do to bring this SR to an end.

However, if it's your soul purpose to do SRs I feel you will enjoy them so much more when gaining some background information, which led to the soul or souls becoming trapped, a little bit like an investigator!

I *love* it!

Through our chat, Nancy and I both felt forgiveness was necessary to bring the curtain down on this (SR), perhaps for not having the strength to withstand our families' issues and taking what sometimes seems the easy way out.

Nancy: *I feel very much at peace, thanks to my dear old Romany sweetheart!*

Me: *Ahh bless you; that's our confirmation that all is well.*

Forgiveness had obviously been offered and accepted by both Nancy's and my soul!

Another SR done – yay!

Swiftly we move on to the next one though, as our conversation continued.

Nancy: *I keep sensing a horse and buggy for some reason.*

Me: *Can you ask your pendulum if this is connected to New York?*

I had a feeling it was but didn't mention it to Nancy, I wanted to see if she got the same vibe from it as I had.

216

Nancy: *Yes, it is!*

Me: *I sense the man was a gentleman a 'lady's man'.*

Nancy: *We were together in New York but I was the man.*

Me: *Wow!*

This surprised me somewhat but throughout our soul's journey it can as easily experience life as a man or woman or animal, bird, etc.!

Nancy: *Yup, sounds like me!*

Me: *I forgive you! I felt I had to say that and also that 'I love you, hope you don't mind?'*

Nancy: *You can say anything to me, after all the lifetimes we have shared and not a dull one it seems, lol! It seems I (the man) forgave you but you (the woman) hadn't as yet forgiven me.*

Me: *This is why I felt the need to tell you that I forgive you and I love you.*

Nancy: *OK, that did it!*

Me: *I feel this lifetime also ended in tragedy.*

Nancy: *Yes, but only I committed suicide in this one.*

Me: *In New York. Does consumption have any meaning?*

Nancy: *Yes, I had consumption (tuberculosis) and killed myself before I suffered any more!*

Me: *Oh wow, I'm filling up here (becoming tearful) and tingling all over!*

I sense in this lifetime, I was unable to forgive, because Nancy, in my eyes, left me, again the issue of loss surfacing!

Through the above conversation I feel peace was brought to this SR but I did ask Archangel Michael that evening to please oversee anything which needed doing to bring either SR to completion.

I woke in the morning and felt a calmness; taking this as a sign that again everything had been dealt with – yay!

Hereditary: An Explanation
An explanation and example:

ANY UNRESOLVED ISSUES our parents, our grandparents, great grandparents, etc., have been unable to bring closure on, will be imprinted onto the next generation, and so on.

So, it isn't the illness which is hereditary, it's the unresolved issue, however if it's the same issue then the illness will most likely be very similar!

For example, my mum and dad were very cautious with money, being very frugal with what they had, living in a 'lack' reality which, when living in a reality like this, money – however much we have – will never ever be enough, whether it's a small or large amount!

Unbeknown to Mum and Dad, they had imprinted on me this same issue regarding money and the lack of it.

So, had I not had the strength to reverse this or any other issues, our souls would have to keep coming back to earth in other forms until these cycles were ended.

During this lifetime, I have been able to bring cycle after cycle to an end, thanks to a vast amount of strength and stubbornness; I get that from Mum and Dad too!

Also, my timely reconnection to God and a wonderful

array of angels who have blessed me with support, strength and Love at the most perfect times, helping me reprogramme my beliefs to the truth of who I *am*.

Rather than the illusion of lack and loss my parents and ancestors were ensconced within, my actions have instigated a healing where any physical ailments which may have started to show up within *me*, can and will be healed completely.

Loss is the fear of losing what we have materially, be it money, loved ones who leave or pass over, friends, our favourite teddy bear, anything we have an attachment to can create a loss issue.

In truth, everything is energy including us, our physical form may change but we never leave because we are all connected so in truth, there really is no such thing as loss.

By ending this specific issue or any other issues I also bring to an end the physical symptoms which have been experienced throughout the challenge of any specific lesson by my parents, grandparents, etc.

Hence, no longer will there be any hereditary issues!

This also explains why there are some people who have a vast amount of money yet still want more, it all stems from a lack belief system.

If you can look at these people and see what money has done to them you can begin to seek out what true happiness really is. Money can buy us temporary happiness. It's one way to help our dreams come true, we can use it to buy equipment, pay bills etc.

When we receive money as payment for doing something we love, we feel more true happiness of the joy of having done this type of 'work' and by helping others in this way, the receipt of money becomes of secondary importance to the work itself; it's a win win situation all round.

What I mean to say is that doing what I love, when I attain the level of having an abundance of money, more than sufficient to live well off, I will gladly do my SR work free or for a donation which will go to a charity.

Who knows, there may well be some who have a large bank account and are truly happy, it is possible!

However, you can have all the money in the world and still be unhappy, the only way to find true happiness is to go within and seek to find who you truly are, to let go of all the illusory beliefs such as lack and fear, and focus on gratitude and thanks for what you have rather than what you don't have.

This is the way to true happiness!

Yvonne, my dear friend, has said to me over the last two years while I've been going through many lessons:

'If you can't be happy with nothing, how can you be happy when you have everything?'

I didn't understand this right away but I do now and the statement is so true.

Over the last few years, I have had a fair amount of money, through the sale of the house when Dad passed. I used it to help me heal on all levels, to give myself time to grieve both Mum and Dad's passing and all that we as a family experienced, until a time it ran out.

So, I've ended up with next to nothing for the last

two years but here's the thing, I still had enough!

I always had a roof over my head, food in my belly, clothes on my back and money in my pocket. OK, it wasn't nearly enough for what I wanted, but until I realised the lesson within the last two years I would not be able to fully appreciate what I had and will have in the future.

Now I make sure I offer thanks and gratitude every day for what I have, for the freedom I have, for the life I have now, focusing on my dreams but being happy with what I have in the present, this is the way to true abundance and prosperity.

I hope this hasn't confused you too much but I felt it was beneficial to share these thoughts!

Another swift example of hereditary is connected with dad, he had three heart attacks within a short space of time and ended up having to have a triple heart by-pass done in the early 1990's, his dad suffered with angina and heart trouble and I dare say this may go back through further generations.

Issues with the heart are associated with feeling unloved, feeling abandoned and the loss of loved ones. I also felt through my life dad didn't love me but I have come to see the truth, he did - he just couldn't bring himself to show it in the way I wanted him to; he did show it in his own way but I have only become aware of it since his passing in 2016.

Each time dad experienced loss he closed his heart off that bit more, feeling the pain, losing loved ones was too much for him to cope with, so he placed a shield if you like around his heart and each time he experienced this pain, the shield grew thicker.

The heart attacks, while very unpleasant began to help dad break down this shield so he could begin to feel the love within himself and for the last few years he was alive, yes it was a very challenging time for both of us, but I know it helped him to begin the process of healing!

The 'Seafarer and His Wife' SR ~ Sometime in 2013 to 18th April 2020

I'M UNSURE WHEN this lifetime was first brought to my attention but I was staying in Whitby around Christmas time.

I have had a few lifetimes to heal in and around Whitby but this one just blew me out of the water, pardon the pun, during an informative chat with Kate, a friend living in the USA.

As the title states, my soul resided within a captain who sailed the world over. On one of his voyages he was killed, never to return home to his beloved wife. As I say, I have done SR work on my soul's experiences in this particular lifetime, which, I have to say have been very emotional indeed, being married to my true love.

However, until this chance meeting on Facebook, not knowing which one of us sent the friend request to ignite this amazing series of events, which have led to this magical outcome for both our souls, but more so for Kate's, as to have that part of her soul freed, to be able to move on makes me so happy!

To explain:

Kate got in touch a few weeks ago, having had no connection since our friend request was accepted. We chatted briefly about various things, my book included. Since then our connection has slowly gained momentum, leading to this amazing conversation on Facebook today.

It is strangely fascinating how we can be gently led into a conversation and then further led to talk about something which has obviously affected us both for many a year, now at the perfect time the issue can and has been brought to a truly remarkable conclusion!

In 2013 I went to Robin Hood's Bay, just a few miles out of Whitby. I went for a walk and paddle in the sea and then went into a Bistro type café for a coffee and a warm! I enjoyed the ambiance; it felt like I was home!

I saw a vision of a gentleman with a beard, wearing a seafaring type cap, smoking a pipe, with the most contented smile upon his face. In this vision he definitely looked like he was in heaven!

I finished my drink and left to head back to Whitby. I thought no more of this vision until a film called *The Captain and Mrs Muir* made in 1947, appeared on TV.

I was curious enough to watch it and wow, I'm so glad I did.

It really blew me away! It was as if this film had been purposely made for me, to see the scenes which would help me bring the lifetime as a seafarer to a perfect end at the perfect time. There was great romance involved too, which I hadn't really thought about!

Without going into too much detail, the film showed the captain and Mrs Muir's life unfold as a seafarer and wife, with a tragic ending. While off on one of his many voyages, the captain's life came to an abrupt end while at sea, never to see his beautiful wife again. When hearing of the captain's death, his wife took it hard and almost wished her life away, forever awaiting his return.

Years pass, Mrs Muir now having aged, sat as she always did, facing the window in hope of the captain's return, but this particular evening as she sat there, glass of milk in her hand, the glass suddenly falls to the floor.

The next scene showed Mrs Muir having slipped away quietly. As I watched this scene unfold, yes, you've guessed it; I was in floods of tears!

At that very same moment, a breeze opened the window and in came the ghost of the captain. He had come back for her, the end scene sees them drifting off over the sea into the mist, so romantic!

This is so similar as to how my soul's lifetime with Kate's played out. I have been able to heal as much of it as I can but until Kate got in touch, this lifetime would still be in limbo, as it were.

I feel that Mrs Muir in the film, as Kate did in the here and now, needed closure.

The fact we were talking about it, able to put the missing pieces together, reuniting our soul connection from that time, was bringing this SR to a very subtle, peaceful conclusion.

Later in the day when I got back in touch with Kate, she said she fell asleep after our chat.

Immediately I got a message from Archangel Michael saying, 'While Kate slept, we were able to 'clear the decks' of all unnecessary emotion, bonds, etc. from this lifetime.'

During her deep sleep, Kate was able to let go of the attachment to her husband in that lifetime – yay!

While sleeping, her husband (my soul) went back to help her soul move on, not as romantic as in the film but it had the same positive effect!

Just to make sure everything was completed I did ask Archangel Michael that if anything needed doing, please do all you can to bring it to a peaceful end, while I slept.

I woke this morning and thought nothing of it, so I take that as a sign all had been resolved during Kate's sleep.

Another amazing experience regarding SR and another slightly different way SRs can be brought to a peaceful and amazing conclusion!

Thank you, Kate, for getting in touch!

Who is Mary? And 'A SR to Boot' ~ 14th April to 26th April 2020

Rather than this being just a SR, it's also an experience I share, because it's such a lovely one and does involve some intuitive work.

I have written about the first paid SR where it was more about me introducing souls in the house who were there to help their loved ones if called upon, as well as involving a SR.

On the Tuesday, I went to get some vitamins from a shop where my dear friend Jody works; while there I picked up a 'hitch hiker' in the form of a soul!

I knew nothing of this until early morning the next day, when awakened by the presence of the soul.

Now this was a soul who wasn't trapped, so was able to move between the two places; Jody's home and mine!

Now, I was going through some deep releasing along with other SR work as well, so it was quite a busy time. If I'm honest, I cut a few corners and immediately asked Archangel Michael to create a portal for this soul to move on, rather than me have a chat with whoever was with me. I just wanted to sleep!

Just going off-piste for a bit!

Moving forward in time to Wednesday 22nd April...

I was vigorously awakened via a dream state!

In the dream I was downstairs with my landlady, feeling a very powerful and unpleasant soul upstairs. I woke, simply because I heard a very loud bang; this was to get my attention, which it did by the way!

It was the presence of a gentleman who I had done work with previously; I thought we had done everything at the time.

We had but as we shed layer upon layer of negativity, through emotions or feelings on behalf of our soul, we go deeper each time, until we reach the core of the matter.

This gentleman had further outstanding issues but from a different lifetime and a different sliver of his trapped soul.

I now feel the unpleasantness within the dream-state was the gentleman's eagerness to move on, he was very frustrated because the other soul involved was unable to let go completely.

I can fully understand how he felt because this has been a challenge for me to accept in the here and now, sometimes I forget we are all on our own unique journey and are doing the best we can, at a pace which suits.

Frustrated or not, things will only happen when the time is perfect; you listening Jeffrey? Mmm, yes!

So, having composed myself, I began to talk to the soul but wasn't getting anywhere. Now, I believe this occurred because my mind was busy with other things. Where once I'd force the questions, this time I stopped and asked Archangel Michael if anything could be done while I slept.

This is helping me learn to be patient and allow the information to flow rather than be forced! Patience will be part of your learning too my friend!

I then got back in bed and went to sleep.

The next morning the same thing happened. I was roused from slumber by two loud noises. I again composed myself and again spoke to the soul and again asked Archangel Michael to do his thing. It was most definitely a *Groundhog Day* experience!

Later in the day, I went for a walk up Rivington, I sat and relaxed my mind sufficiently for a thought to surface: *do a SR while here*.

By this time I had realised the two souls involved were both with me! This time, completion attained!

The reason this had taken so long to heal was because the lady's soul, however painful the experience, couldn't let go of the male; she loved him in that lifetime, regardless of his actions.

I too had a lot on my plate and was unable to give it my full attention. However, as I keep being reminded: everything is in divine and perfect order!

This may well occur during your journey as a soul retriever, if this is your purpose, be gentle because it's all a part of the remembering process.

I did exactly what was meant to be done, on each occasion this gentleman woke me up, ending with a wonderful experience for them both in a lovely setting; perfect!

Having dealt with this SR, unbeknown to me Mary was now able to make herself clearly felt, and very soon – 25th April Saturday morning, at 4.56am, to be precise!

I chatted with Jody on Friday evening, when

eventually our chat focused on her sons Tom, but more so Luke, who is very connected in a spiritual way; he converses with souls, feels them, etc. Jody told me the name of a lady who is frequently around Luke, her name: Mary! I completely forgot about Mary's connection with me the other day while in the shop.

Jody told me that Mary wakes her up very early every morning to hear the birds singing, finding it a tad annoying but in the nicest way possible; Jody is a very pure hearted soul. One of Mary's loves is that of listening to the birds sing.

Our conversation ended as bedtime approached.

Early Saturday morning, I was again roused from slumber by a noise, not as loud as the previous early morning wake-up calls!

Within a minute of composing myself, I heard the birds singing outside my window. So, being reminded of my chat with Jody the night before, I asked the soul, 'Is it you Mary?' The reply came in an instant!

The light in my salt lamp flickered and I went tingly all over; a definite yes!

I then asked:

Are you ready to move on?

I felt no energy change, etc., so I took that as a 'no'.

Are you watching over Luke, as a guardian angel or spirit guide?

The answer I received was a definite 'yes'!

Are you a relation of Jody's, her grandmother or great-grandmother?

I got a bit giddy when asking Mary this.

I left very little time for her to answer, so didn't get clarity but as it turns out I felt it was the latter.

I felt I had asked enough questions, so I thanked Mary for being here, then I went back to sleep.

Later in the day I messaged Jody and asked:

Do you have any relations, grandmother or great-grandmother named Mary?

Jody said she had a great aunt and a great-grandmother she had never met; again, further confirmation for me – yay!

I told Jody about my experience, especially about the timing, from when I woke up to the birds singing, not really having an idea how she would take it but I needn't have worried.

Jody's reply:

Awwww, that's amazing!

I know I have Mary in my house who adores birds and I did wonder if she was my great-aunt but she's never answered when I've asked, so it's just beautiful to have confirmation, thank you xxxx.

When I read this I felt a tad relieved, because of the other goings-on but how things play out. To have played a part in connecting Jody to her relative has been a pleasure!

Having brought the SR to an end, it then allowed Mary to remind Jody she was still around.

My mind de-cluttered from all those emotions surrounding the SR, being able then to focus on Mary and to help Jody and her sons receive confirmation, is just so heart warming.

I know but I'm going to say it again: this is why I so *love* doing SRs in these magical ways. I am *so* blessed!

The 'Wooded Mound' SR ~ 25th April 2020 – Start & Finish!

ON THE 25TH April, during the writing of the previous piece, I went for a walk near to where I live at the moment, which took me through a small raised wooded area.

I had no idea but Archangel Michael asked me to prepare to do a SR while there!

I did as I was asked, circling as much of the raised mound where the trees are, inviting any souls there to allow themselves to be helped to move on as I would normally.

As I walked around the top of the mound, I came across quite a few pristine white feathers, maybe eight in total. (White feathers appear when we seek a sign from our loved ones, that they or angels are very close and hearing our prayers.) However, I understood each feather to be a symbol of a soul who had been trapped there for however long!

This too was a nice touch, confirmation in a different way!

Almost at the end of the SR I was invited by Archangel

Michael to 'open' myself, so he could step into my body, radiating his light out into the area through me.

This really blew me away!

I had no prior knowledge this would happen but again it's another succinct way these amazing SRs can be completed.

Dora (Mum) and William (Me) SR ~ 4th May 2020

WHERE TO START?

This may be a longer piece than the others but I do feel it will be worth me adding this SR because it ties up so many loose ends for me and my beloved mum's soul.

Yet another experience which blew me away!

28th April 2020

I have recently been reacquainted with Tania, a beautiful soul from Australia.

During our first chat, Tania was already channelling messages, passing those she felt conducive to our chat, on to me.

With Tania's help, we brought an ancestral issue of Mum's to an end, which goes back I don't know how far but it has had a negative effect on me, too.

The topic: love/sex...

Mum was made to feel, when she either mentioned or partook in this experience, that it was 'dirty'. I feel this goes back to some religious experience which has caused this whole issue! Her grandmother had over a period of time brainwashed Mum into believing this was fact.

This has had an effect on me and the way I was introduced to this issue, but through this chat with Tania I was able to heal any rift between me, Mum and my great-grandmother, and hopefully all the way back to the moment this issue originated; happy days!

So, a 'mini' SR occurred and peace brought to all involved – yay!

That was the starter course.
Now for the main, dessert, coffee and biscuit courses!

Tania and I swiftly move on to our next port of call. Tania told me about a lifetime which has had recurring experiences for her in this life, during our chat we were able to bring some peace to Tania and the other souls involved.

Tania then described a lifetime we experienced together. Her initial comment: 'I'm seeing a library', saying the library was mine, old and dusty but beautiful.

Having read the message, I instinctively replied: 'Was it Dove Cottage?'

Tania: *Oh my gosh, my stomach flipped when you said that.*

It had a thatch-like roof.

Brown beams and a garden of ivy, it was a wild, unkempt garden.

Me: *It's where William Wordsworth once lived. I visited there a few years ago and when I went into the room where the chaise longue sofa was I went tingly all over. I feel my soul was Wordsworth!*

Indeed, I felt a connection to this house the whole

way through it, it had a warm, comforting feeling but in this particular room the tingling went to another level!

Tania: *When you said Dove Cottage, I saw it as a snapshot.*

Oh yes you were! (referring to my soul being Wordsworth)

Tania then described the house, saying again that I didn't mind the unkempt gardens, and the cottage's exterior was white and brown. Adding that William/my soul didn't go out much – the same can be said of me now in this lifetime, I do love my own company!

I felt guided to send Tania a picture of the cottage. Having done so, this was her reply:

Tania: *I thank my angels and my guides this is the house I saw when you said Dove Cottage.*

I got goose bumps.

I have been there.

I know that place well.

White and brown.

As I read the steady in-flow of messages, I said that I too was going goose bumpy all over. Definite signs the truth was being shown to us by our angelic friends!

Tania then sent me a picture of the house she saw in her vision. She then posted another batch of messages, which appeared on our chat page.

Tania: *High windows*

White and brown.

Ivy up the side.

Jeffrey, thank you.

I was there too.

I feel absolutely thrilled.

What was my name? I know I was a female.

I can't pick my name up.

Was I Sarah or Mary?
I don't know!

By this time, it was getting late; for Tania, almost midnight. I started to search for information that would bring her name to our awareness. I mentioned two names: Elizabeth and Isabella.

Tania's reply was again staggering!

Tania: *Isabella. That sounds right.*

Elizabeth didn't. Wait, Isabella isn't sitting so well!

I felt by this time I was trying to force the issue, trying to find the name of Tania's soul in this lifetime but now I had the wisdom to say let's leave the rest for another day. Tania agreed.

We said good night and left it perfectly poised for the outcome to be attained at a later date.

Saturday, 2nd May 2020:

Tania and I resume to bring closure to a truly amazing passage of our past-life connection. So, many pieces of the jigsaw coming together at the most opportune and perfect time for Tania's, my mum's and my soul.

I will say this again: God and our angelic friends from all realms do work in very mysterious and truly magical ways!

Me: *Does the name Dorothy or Mary resonate with you?*

Tania: *Mary resonates more out of the two.*

Tania's soul was indeed Mary, Wordsworth's wife!

I told Tania about Wordsworth and that Mary was his wife; that they had five children but two predeceased them; Dove Cottage was their first home from 1808 to 1811, when they then moved to Allan Bank for two years before finally settling at Rydal Mount in 1813 until

William died in 1850, followed by Mary in 1859.

The first two houses are more important simply because I have visited them, the other house I haven't as yet been guided to.

Rydal Mount was the first house I visited, around four years ago.

I did the tour of the house and grounds. It felt heavy with sadness and grief, but more so in the grounds themselves; I was brought to tears while walking the grounds and sitting on the bench which overlooks a lake.

One thing which I do remember now was that I felt a strong connection to 'Dora' his daughter while walking through the gardens but it didn't really mean anything at the time.

Now, my visit occurred just before I fully understood about SR work, so I had no idea what or whom I was connecting with, just as my initiation to SR work had occurred at Whitby.

Now I know I was connecting to the essences of emotions and a trapped part of my soul during the visit.

I then visited Dove Cottage a short while after, feeling very warm and comforting, a different atmosphere all together! As I have said about the room with the chaise longue, when I looked at the sofa being told it was where Wordsworth wrote some of his work, I went very tingly all over.

I relayed this information to Tania in the hope it would spark some other insight from her. It did, giving her such a clear vision of the house and in part why we had very recently reconnected via Facebook to unravel this particular lifetime our souls had been part of, Mum's, too.

As I mentioned Dora I went tingly all over, a sign she was there, making herself known to me. For confirmation, I asked Tania if she could sense Dora around me.

Tania wasn't able to give me a 'Yes' or 'No' but by the time Tania replied I knew it was for me to trust what I sensed and felt. I started to feel very emotional and that my soul/William hadn't fully let go of Dora, this is what needed to be attended to via SR.

Dora was with me!

Tania: *She was a small girl/woman I feel, Jeffrey, and had dark hair.*

She wore a kind of pinafore.

Some sort of black undergarment.

But I feel she had trouble with her legs!

The strong connection I felt with Dora turned out to be a very close and special one, as I found out via Tania's channelled messages.

Dora suffered with frequent ill health, whereupon she passed in 1847 due to TB (tuberculosis).

Tania: *I wonder if that affected her legs?*

I feel she had trouble moving them in the end.

I did a spot of research and found that TB of the spine can cause back pain and leg paralysis.

Tania: *Oh, gee that gives me absolute chills (confirmation).*

She (Dora) showed me her legs, they were very swollen with fluid.

Hard to move, stiff.

I say she had TB of the spine,

William carries her,
No wonder you have a hard time letting go!
Both of you do.
But I feel more William.

Having read the messages as they came through, I was overcome with emotion. A thought entered from nowhere.

My mum in this life, her soul was Dora – in one amazing moment it all made sense!

Mum in this life had had cancer for over twenty years and other ailments but her legs were a mess. I would massage her legs with cream but they were so hard, swollen, no circulation getting through to her feet. Like I say, her legs were a mess, as indeed was her whole body!

I was quite emotional at this insight 'No wonder I have had, as you said "mother issues to deal with"' – a message which Tania had sent me a week or so ago!

Tania: *Oh yes indeed; she carried the leg thing over!*

Me: *Ah, thank you so much for helping me to get to the bottom of this, it makes so much sense and guess what?*

It's Mum's birthday tomorrow, 3rd May.

How perfectly timed!

Tania: *Dora passed with the issue unhealed.*

Oh gosh that is perfect!

Me: *Since my panic attack and learning Reiki, I was able to help Mum heal and eventually pass in peace, without knowing what I was really doing.*

Mum came through time and time again during healings I have had with Yvonne and many times did she say, 'You have done everything you could.'

I have understood some of what Mum said but

not until this very moment did I fully understand what happened as Mum's illness deteriorated. The other hidden blessings within my panic attack, which instigated this whole process of our healing:

Both Mum and my soul can now rest much more easily after this enlightenment, which has been priceless on many levels.

One blessing, is that yes, my soul was a famous writer in this past lifetime, but to have had the help from Tania and her psychic gifts, even I can no longer doubt my soul has experienced lifetimes in famous bodies as other souls have; there have been way too many coincidences.

Yvonne first began to tell me what had happened during our many magical healing sessions together, when unravelling who my soul had lived as and experienced life through, the various bodies of both the famous and wealthy, and the ordinary people.

I now thank Yvonne for sharing this priceless information, without which I would have struggled immeasurably in attaining this level of understanding regarding my soul purpose, my SR work and writing – thank you!

It has *never* been about who my soul was; it's about what my soul experienced and that in this present lifetime what *we*, Jeffrey and Shanti, can do to help each other heal our past experiences.

Jeffrey... Healing his ancestral issues

Shanti... Healing his many, varied sojourns to this world!

The act of doing the SR for this experience happened during the unveiling of the information, a remarkable and beautiful way for all trapped souls to move on, the letting go part has also been done without my realising it was happening, such was the subtlety of my SR teammates.

Bless you, one and all!

4th May 2020

I really thought we had done everything yesterday on Mum's birthday, 3rd May. Ah, what do I know!

This afternoon I visit Rivington for a walk; much needed after the last few days.

I felt the emotions which were about to surface needed to be 'walked out' to some degree, so I walked further than usual, then went to sit on the bench I have frequented over the last few weeks.

Bare feet placed flat on the ground, relaxing, allowing the elements to wash over me. Within minutes I had a thought to ask Archangel Michael to create a portal of light, just in case there were any souls hereabout ready to move on.

Little did I know two of the souls would be those of Dora (Mum's) and William (my soul) trapped in this lifetime!

I then heard a voice saying, 'They have gone together.' I took this to mean both Dora's and William's souls had moved on.

They did so hand-in-hand, a perfect way to end a perfect experience but it does, in my view, show how hard it was to let go of this lifetime!

Finally, the SR completed in a beautiful setting, which was also very apt!

Triceratops SR ~ Circa Sixty Million Years Ago (give or take a year!) to Present!

THIS PAST-LIFE SR issue was brought to me unexpectedly, to say the least.

I was booked in to have a healing with Yvonne on the 6th March 2018. During the healing I was shown a scene from the dinosaur era; very strange I thought, but went with it. It opened up to show my soul as a Triceratops baby being chased and bitten into by a Tyrannosaurus rex (T. rex).

When the healing finished, I asked Yvonne, 'Did you go into a dinosaur lifetime?' The reply was a simple, 'No.'

However, by the time I was ready to leave Yvonne's, I knew it was for me to trust and receive the information as and when it came through.

It was much easier at the time to trust, with it coming to me at Yvonne's, had it come while I was elsewhere it would have been much harder to trust.

Had a SR taken place when in receipt of this first vision?

I honestly don't think so, I feel it was giving me an

opportunity to experience this first-hand from beginning to end, trusting everything I received.

An invaluable experience as it has turned out. This has been a challenge at times but I have done it – yay!

My first realisation was this must be one of, if not the first, visit to earth for Shanti, my soul!

The scene I was blessed with was the instigator of all Shanti's experiences here during his many, many visits since.

This was a pivotal moment, when the T. rex took a chunk out of the Triceratops baby, more specifically his bottom.

This one instance caused the emotions to flow, emotions until this one moment, the baby hadn't experienced.

In truth, however long the baby had been on earth, it was a very sedate, tranquil one, until all hell broke loose with the aid of not one but a group of T. rex who were on the hunt for food!

One thing that has emerged over a period of time regarding this lifetime came when Yvonne told me I hadn't forgiven the soul of the T. rex; understandable I suppose! So, this was one aspect I needed to work on and has taken a while to completely forgive, if I'm honest!

Also, it became clear I needed to thank the T. rex's soul (who at this moment in time resides within a good friend of mine) for she sparked me into action regarding my spiritual journey on earth. Had this seemingly abhorrent experience not occurred, my soul may still be munching on the vegetation blissfully unaware of the many emotions/experiences he was missing out on.

When/if you do find the origin of your soul's first visit to earth and begin to understand what instigated your soul's journey into these unpleasant feelings/emotions, it is for you to thank the souls who caused your situation.

Knowing what I/we do now, we would gladly erase all those unpleasant experiences, however they are part and parcel of life, we have to experience both sides of the coin to understand what life on earth is all about!

What my soul experienced in that one moment changed his whole life and journey on earth.

The emotions which surfaced:
Shock: Not expecting anything like that to happen!
Fear: Having been struck once and being rendered incapacitated, he was a sitting duck for further attacks, and however long this took, fear would have escalated until death.
Pain: As the teeth sank in, this, again, is a shocking new feeling to experience.
Loss/abandonment: Being separated from his family and more so when they didn't come back to help him! (Perhaps seeing a loved one being eaten, too?)
Anger/frustration: Why did no other family member come to help?
Confusion/panic: At the initial moment the teeth sank in, it caused chaos for all dinosaurs in the vicinity, not only my soul's body.

What had the baby (my soul) done to deserve this?
What had he done wrong?
And why me?

That second question has haunted me ever since I learnt about this lifetime. Because in every lifetime I have been back into, there has been a situation where I have asked the same question over and over.

The simple answer to this question: I/my soul has never done anything wrong, ever!

It's similar to the experience Adam and Eve had, when Eve supposedly bit into the poisoned apple. This I now see as a metaphor for the instigation of their and our many earth experiences which have encompassed every emotion God has created.

Had Adam and Eve not partaken of the proverbial forbidden fruit experience, there would have been no earth experiences; some may say that would have been a blessing, me included at various times in my life!

However, everything that has happened on earth, in my belief, stems from that one action.

Every soul who has visited this world has experienced a moment like this, maybe not exactly the same but a scenario which would ignite all those feelings and emotions not yet experienced by your soul.

So, how has the SR been completed...

Well, the person the T. rex's soul resides in, in this lifetime, actually gave me shelter when I was homeless.

We were obviously brought together in this way to heal our differences.

Our souls have had other lifetimes together causing each to experience many emotions both good & bad, so for the duration I stayed with this person we had been given ample time to bring our karma into balance.

Through our chats about this lifetime and others, forgiveness was the key to our healing and balancing our karma.

I also feel this SR has been achieved over a period of time through visits while I/Jeffrey slept, with the additional information coming along at the perfect time, so the healing could be carried out at intervals.

Our physical body can only cope with so much healing at once; it then needs rest before the next healing phase, and so on.

The forgiveness came as I understood more as time passed, and indeed by the time I left my friends home, absolute forgiveness had been attained on both sides.

I know it isn't a 'full-on' SR but it will help you, when opening up to your soul's past, to be able to do SR for yourself, to access the information you need, help you release and forgive both yourself and others.

With this wisdom you are perfectly placed to help others through your experiences, and so on!

The 'Gentle Giant' SR ~ 25th May to 5th October 2020

THIS HAS BEEN in the process of coming into my consciousness for a few months but only now has it been made clear and boy what an amazing experience!

Throughout the period of this SR I have been blessed with many opportunities where my buttons have been well and truly pressed, sometimes quite uncomfortably so.

Each time, anger has been at the forefront of emotions to surface.

This goes back into a past life where a part of my soul/Shanti was a 'giant' – a term given because of the height difference, obviously, but in truth he was only two feet taller than some, the height difference a little more with others but it was enough to have caused him great heartache during his life.

I was shown a picture of these giants in a photo with ordinary people, if you like, living in the community together but it wasn't always the case, as I'm about to tell you.

My soul, the giant, was a very sensitive soul, as I feel most of them were but their size opened them up to all sorts of abuse; this is what my soul experienced.

Yesterday I watched a film version of *King Kong* and right at the end someone said, 'It was beauty that killed the beast.' This upset me slightly but this was only the start of an amazing unveiling of this lifetime I now tell you of.

Back to the giant...

'Beauty' was a woman who was indeed beautiful but chose to ridicule the giant at any opportunity; this led to the whole community following her lead.

'Beast', the giant, being sensitive, took these hurtful words to heart, he retreated within himself to the point of becoming numb and indeed paranoid, leading to a life of solitude, passing with a broken heart not knowing what he had done wrong.

Fast forward to this present lifetime and Jeffrey (me).

When I/Jeffrey, was at secondary school I was almost the tallest in the school but I was in the first year, aged eleven. As is the case with some children, they taunt those who are different. Those who don't want to be targeted in this way will be somewhat forced to join their gang, if you will. I was obviously a target, more so from the girls.

When it started, each night I would go home, have my tea and cry into my pillow because of the name calling, etc. After a while I became numb, oblivious to their name calling, however, I distanced myself and soon became paranoid, so much so it affected my adult life, too.

A few years ago, I went to a school reunion; believe me I would have rather done anything else but I felt I needed to bring an end to the treatment I received while at school. I went and everything went better than expected. I came to realise that, after all they were just children as I was, so I was able to forgive them and let go of this part of my life.

Are you noticing any similarities between the giant and Jeffrey?

Well, this is the magical part.

As I have mentioned in a SR earlier in this book, I had an experience whereby a walk-in came into my body.

A soul entered and a soul left, in one swift movement, and I felt nothing, no change in life, nothing.

However, this experience did change my life, for at that moment the Shanti part came in and began to guide many changes within my life.

Shanti chose to reside within me because of my experiences since childbirth in this present lifetime, including the ridiculing Jeffrey experienced as a child, teenager and perhaps adult too!

Now, I believe I had these experiences as a child, to prepare me for the time when Shanti moved in, to help him release and reconnect with all the parts of his soul which had become trapped since his earth journey began.

Although it was an unpleasant time at school, I now know there was a reason behind it and now I'm just so glad I've been an able body for my soul/Shanti to do his work through me.

Going back to the film, *King Kong*...

Having understood the message, it wasn't long before

the vision of the photo entered my mind.

Things started to come together like a jigsaw, until I had all the pieces and was then able to piece them together.

The soul of the woman who ridiculed the giant's soul is someone very close within my reality at this time, they don't know anything about what I've been going through, and hopefully they won't mind if they ever read this and put two and two together!

In truth, this soul has been of great help to me and to their own journey because all the unpleasantness, the emotions experienced by both our souls over a very long period, each and every one needs to be healed, accepted, released and forgiveness attained, on both sides.

Until this happens, both our souls will continuously be brought opportunities until we finally complete this cycle; I dare say after this lifetime we are almost, if not fully complete, regarding our karma.

The final act: when all this information came to light and having pieced it together, I was then blessed with a reminder of how it felt in that lifetime as a giant and in this present lifetime also as a giant, as I stand at 6ft 7ins.

I know it isn't the tallest in the world but it has been all part of my soul's plan to recreate as much of this past life as possible, so when the time came I/Jeffrey would know exactly what was going on and what I was feeling and being asked to release on my soul's behalf.

I was in the kitchen when the realisation kicked-in!

I felt the hurt and the pain of every word the woman said and what she did, the other people in the community, what they said and did, and the accumulated hurt and pain Jeffrey has experienced in this lifetime all came up at once.

Well, tears flowed, to experience those feelings I had locked up inside of me/Jeffrey at that force was quite a shock, to be honest!

But I am so grateful to everyone who has played their part in bringing these feelings up.

The SR can now take place. I feel it will be a SR that I know little about, as it will happen while Jeffrey is asleep but that's fine, the main thing is, the SR can now be completed, forgiveness offered and now it's time to move on.

For my soul in that lifetime I felt he was so heartbroken, he committed suicide and as you know when this happens a soul can become easily trapped by the different emotions he was experiencing, which all lead to fear.

This has helped me/Jeffrey release so much via emotions, such as:

A deep lack of self-worth ~ because *I am worthy*.

What have I done wrong? ~ I did nothing wrong; people sometimes fear anything which is remotely different to what's in their reality, their comfort zone.

And a fear of being unloved ~ because *I am loved*.

This whole experience has been a blessed gift. I have felt another great weight lift from my shoulders, now able to move on to experience life as I deserve it to be, full of everything that I love doing!

There have been no new ways of doing SR added here but here is the point of Soul Retrieval, it's all about helping the trapped soul(s) move on. It's as important to understand what had caused the soul to become trapped, especially if it's part of your soul's journey.

When given information as I have been blessed with, it makes the forgiving easier, the releasing easier; the moving on for the soul in the present to move on easier, too.

This is all part of our soul's journey: to reconnect to those trapped parts of our soul through SR with the existing main part of our soul which is in another realm, having experiences at a higher conscious level. This is the aim of all souls who visit this planet for what I call 'The Earth Experience'!

SR completion.
On the 1st October 2020. I had the most amazing healing with Yvonne, which brought up so much to work on, regarding forgiveness of others and myself too.

It's Saturday 3rd October 2020, and as I read the above SR, I realise part of the healing on Thursday was connected to this specific SR.

If I may explain, during the healing a soul made himself known to Yvonne as we chatted. I was told this soul had appeared before but only now does he understand the issue behind him being trapped.

He committed suicide as the giant did, but the issue which trapped him was fear and how he had allowed it to affect his life and indeed affecting my soul's journey since then, until now.

The soul who moved on during the healing was the Giant, wow. Now. having understood this as I read it, I can now fully release, let go and forgive all involved with this SR bringing it to a very timely closure.

And yes I will say it yet again, amazing!

It's now the 5th October 2020 and I feel I'm definitely in the final throes of bringing this issue and SR to complete and utter closure, fingers crossed!

The Giant was a child and the soul who was "Beauty" in this lifetime was also a child (this now makes so much sense) this brings about an amazing piece of knowledge which will add to your understanding of SR too.

As I have written previously, my soul, Shanti walked-in in 1999. I/Jeffrey, as a child had issues at school being so tall, being called names etc., to the point I became paranoid.

This SR has now been shown to me to be a priceless experience, for having experienced this unpleasantness as a child, I am now able to connect to and understand the feelings Shanti experienced during his lifetime as the Giant and many other lifetimes which led to this issue being brought up to be attended to.

I am now able to surrender and let go of these emotions on behalf of Shanti through my physical body and childhood experiences. Sometimes forgiving can take a little longer depending on the experience, so please don't beat yourself up if you can't seem to forgive everyone instantly, after all we are human!

It's another example how your physical body and its experiences, will complement your soul's healing journey, so you can clear your ancestral issues and your soul can heal his/her issues too!

A perfect example of Team work, this SR will definitely be brought to a truly magical conclusion throughout today.

Do I need to say it?
Amazing!

Druid's Temple - Ripon (SR & EC) ~ 5th July 2020

(This is an eleventh hour addition, while Catherine and her team at 2QT have already begun to sift through the manuscript of this book. However, I do feel this piece is necessary for the priceless gifts I have again been blessed with.)

Today is the full moon in conjunction with an eclipse occurring, so it's a powerful time energetically for all.

Debbie, Jo and I set off for the temple very early morning, 4am, arriving around 6am.

At the site I immediately felt guided to go off to the left and further guided until I came upon a gap in the trees, leading me to a most wondrous sight.

Facing me was a valley, a reservoir, fields and a railway bridge in the far distance but the main star of the show was a truly beautiful rainbow, so brightly coloured, I've never seen a rainbow as radiant! Having feasted on the beauty of this picturesque scene, I made my way back to the temple.

I entered the temple and saw before me a large, square block of stone, feeling something untoward had happened here! So, I called upon my SR teammates, inviting them to assist me with whatever was here in soul form.

The temple itself is around one hundred feet long and maybe thirty feet at its widest, with a small covered building at the opposite end to the entrance. I received guidance to place Reiki symbols into the stones and ground as I walked clockwise around the temple.

At the other end of the circle, I walked through a doorway and around a large stone slab, before entering the cave-type building, again placing symbols into the area. Heading back to the entrance I sensed a soul at the doorway where the slab was! I felt the need to continue to walk around the inner of the temple before being guided back to the doorway.

Now back at the doorway.

I walk through the doorway and again I felt a soul's energy.

I did this a few times talking to him all the while, asking him to allow this portal of energetic light to help him move on.

Stepping through the doorway for a fourth time, I felt no energy, I took this as confirmation the soul had moved on.

I then moved to the entrance and finished the SR by asking my teammates to bless this area with their own divine gifts.

That was it; we got back to the car, and set off towards home!

However, the real magic of this SR appeared hours later while I rested on my bed.

I felt there had been unpleasant experiences in this

temple but I had slightly misinterpreted the signs. I received information that the square block of stone near the entrance had at some point in its journey been the platform for ritual sacrifice before arriving at the temple!

I had picked up on the essences of those who were sacrificed on the altar stone and what I was being invited to do was to cleanse and clear the stone of all those emotions/memories which had seeped into it; hence the symbols.

In addition, the soul I briefly connected with at the doorway, his energies were very gentle yet filled with peace and contentment, I feel this is the reason he didn't want to leave, bless him!

Having received these two pieces of information, it put a whole new look on this SR, giving me another piece of priceless information regarding the structure of this and any other place I visit to do SR work!

In this example a stone which had come from somewhere else had carried with it the memories/ emotions of souls sacrificed upon it, who may still be trapped in the place where the stone once stood.

Hmmm, another SR for me to do?

All I can say again, is, amazing!

Soul Retriever's 'Toolkit'
(Guidelines)

LISTEN AT ALL times to your intuition!

Build your energy up by doing small SRs before even thinking about diving into the dark/black magic SRs.

This may well be your path to deal with the dark SRs but please take it step by step as I have been guided to do.

Being attuned to any healing modalities such as any form of Reiki, Shamanic or crystal healing etc. will help elevate your vibration to a level where you can cope with the challenges the SRs involving negative/dark energies may gift you.

In addition, as we raise our vibration, we will receive occasional downloads/ activations during sleep or meditation too.

Protection:

Calling on your angels.

Using any healing symbols you have been attuned to.

Rock salt/Ordinary salt: If you are doing a SR which involves unpleasant energies it's wise to encircle yourself with the salt so that as you begin your SR calling in your guides, etc. you will have added protection!

Sage: To cleanse the area, especially inside a building of any type!

Holy water: To cleanse the area, outside! If you have no Holy water, simply ask God to bless any water you have at hand.

Crystals: There are crystals which can be used as an added protection for you depending on the nature of the SR, such as Pyrite, Shungite, Black Tourmaline, Black Obsidian and there are others, or ask to be guided to the perfect crystals, by your guides!

Prayers: The Lord's Prayer or any prayer which you feel may be apt for the SR you are working on.

Talk to the souls in a gentle manner, be empathetic to their situation, however they became trapped. If there are two or more souls involved share with them your knowledge regarding forgiveness, because forgiveness in any situation is the Key to freedom!

Respect each soul you connect with!
Be fearless but sensible!
And more importantly: *enjoy* the experiences!

Lightning Source UK Ltd.
Milton Keynes UK
UKHW021306260821
389503UK00004B/37

9 781913 071875